The Pikes Peak Region Scouting Story

100 Years

1916--2016

Intro by Kent Downing

Pikes Peak Council Scout Executive

Since 1916, the Pikes Peak Council, Boy Scouts of America has been the regions foremost program of character development and values-based leadership training for youth. The program encourages youth to pursue their special interests, make new friends, develop leadership skills, and give back to their community. Annually, Scouting serves the needs of nearly 10,000 local youth and adult mentors and over the past 100 years, hundreds of thousands of individuals have been positively impacted by the program. I would like to offer a special thank you to the 100th Anniversary History Committee, for leading the effort to create this publication documenting the history of this great council. We hope you enjoy learning about Scouting's "Century of Adventure" in the Pikes Peak region!

Kent Downing	Brian Bahr	Steve Hayes
Scout Executive	Council President	Council Commissioner

Disclaimer

Information for this booklet has been obtained from internet, libraries, old newspapers, word of mouth, Scout lore, old scouters and anywhere else we could find it. We do not guarantee the accuracy of this pamphlet and if we miss identified something or someone, we are sorry. Following the Scout moto, we tried to do our best.

For any of you old scouters out there, if you have facts or stories about the council please pass them to the council and they will forward them to me for possible revisions to the book.

History committee comprised of David L. Krzemien, Jim Yagmin, Barb Sweat and John H. Brown (Chairperson)

Editor and researcher: John H. Brown

"The Beginning"

10/17/1910 – A few weeks ago a meeting was held in this city by a number of people interested in the Boy Scout movement. At that meeting a committee was named for the purpose of organizing Boy Scout Patrols in Colorado Springs and vicinity.

Mr. R. H. Arnold, Mr. F. M. Maris and Mr. A. J. Yeomans, formed a committee to see the city's interest in the movement and let the committee know there interest and would they be willing to help.

Anyone desiring information and full details regarding rules, regulations, etc., one should get the "Boy Scout Manual," which may be bought for 30 cents.

*Article printed in the Colorado Springs Gazette in October 1910.

C. M. Balkam, an early Scouting supporter, in a letter to the Colorado Springs Gazette in March 1911 stated, "Robust, and manly, self-reliant boyhood" has changed into "a lot of flat-chested cigarette smokers with shaky nerves and doubtful ability."

"The nation is showing signs of illness. We can diagnose it as 'bad citizenship.' We know the kind of remedy to apply, namely education of the rising generation in 'character'. When there was snow on the ground in Colorado Springs, it wasn't safe to go outside for fear of being pelted by snowballs. Boys would jump onto cars on the street "no matter how many casualties happened," wrote F. Beyle in 1911. "Broken windows, damaged tombstones, stolen chickens, coal and wood – all were blamed on rowdy boys. "

All that was needed to organize a Scout Patrol was finding a scoutmaster willing to give one night a week and 10 days at summer camp. Get a committee appointed and some assistants.

"WE NEED SCOUTING"

Pikes Peak Council Scouting History

1916 to 1925

As with everything in the Colorado Springs area things take time to gel into a solid organization. The Scouting movement started with a visitor from England who came to Colorado Springs for the beauty of the area and his health. With the help of his brother from Kansas, Dr. G. E. Romanes and F. John Romanes saw the need for scouting in the area and organized a meeting of parents and their sons. The meeting was held in the Steele School in September 1910 and was attended by twenty boys and their parents. The first patrol was organized by F. John Romanes, (National Commissioner) and a parent committee was formed to be in charge of the Scout extension work in Colorado Springs and the region. F. John Romanes was from Salina, Kansas, and was an instructor at St. John's Military School.

Following closely in October, 1910, a second patrol was organized under the leadership of the Boys Department of the Y.M.C.A. This was an exciting time for Scouting and it caught on like wild fire. In April, 1911, the Gazette stated that ten patrols had been organized and were doing well.

Patrol 4 Colorado Springs

In 1911 Colorado Springs Boy Scouts filed with Colorado for incorporation with 10 patrols. The Colorado Springs Council was founded in 1916, and in 1922 changed its name to the El Paso and Teller Counties Council.

1917

In March, 1917, a meeting was held for reorganization and improvement of Scouting in Colorado Springs with Mr. Ludwig S. Dale (National Field Scout Commissioner for the Rocky Mountain region) in attendance, plus a number of prominent business men who pledged their assistance in the reorganization. It was anticipated that a permanent Scout Executive would be employed. The meeting concluded with teams of members appointed to fund raise for the Scouting effort. A budget of $8,000 was the goal and in August, 1917, they came up just short by $25, but one of the volunteers made up the amount. The first Scout Executive was hired August, 1917, that being Homer J. Bemiss from San Francisco and the headquarters was set up in the Out West building, room 17 for the rent of $10 per month.

Pikes Peak Council is home to the oldest continually-chartered troop in the state of Colorado, Troop 2, originally chartered to Colorado Springs' First Presbyterian Church in October, 1917 with nine Scouts—sixteen months after the Boy Scouts of America was first chartered by the United States Congress 15 June, 1916. Troop 2 is the oldest mission of the church.

Scouting's full resources were placed at the service of the government when we entered WWI.

Slogan: "Help Win the War".

1918

Due to his wife's health Mr. Bemiss resigned and Mr. Earl B. Moore, Scoutmaster of Troop 7 was appointed Scout Executive taking over his duties on 1 April 1918. The following week, Camp Vigil, at the head of Little Fountain Creek, was offered to the local scout committee as a permanent summer camp. The site was leased for three years. The first summer camp lasted four days and 44 boys attended, hiking all the way from the Broadmoor Hotel. In 1923, Spencer Penrose bought a 16-acre camp in Pike National Forest, eight miles from his beloved Broadmoor, and built some cabins there to create an outdoor vacation experience. He planned to sell memberships, but instead had a great time entertaining his friends for summer getaways. He called his personal retreat Camp Vigil.

BSA adopted the slogan "The War Is Over, but Our Work Is Not".

The boys were participating in the first Liberty Loan drive and the local Scouts sold $10,000 worth of bonds and four medals were awarded for the boys' efforts. A second Liberty Loan drive was held and the Scouts sold 430 bonds having a value of $80,350. Twenty boys were successful in selling over ten bonds each. Medals were awarded to Scouts selling over ten bonds. The third drive raised $31,150 and the fourth raising $71,950. Over 300 boys took part in these drives and 100 of them won medals for securing 10 or more pledges.

Scouting's full resources were placed at the service of the government as part of the war effort. From 1917 to 1918, Scouts sold 2,350,977 Liberty Loan bonds, totaling $147,876,902; and war savings stamps, to a value of $53,043,698. More than 300 million pieces of government literature were distributed, and services rendered included food and fuel conservation and Boy Scout war gardens.

In June 1917, the total enrollment was 103 boys in five troops. By August 1918, the enrollment had jumped to 340 Scouts and 17 troops.

1919

On December, 1919 the Scout Executive showed there were 13 troops, and 247 active scouters.

The Rotary Club on 19 December appropriated a sum up to $1,500 to build a camp in Bear Creek Canyon. The cabin was completed in March 1920 and the camp was named Camp Vessey* in honor of Bernard Vessey of the Rotary Club. Mr. Vessey was a song leader of the Colorado Springs Rotary Club.

For 30 years it was in use, both winter and summer, as a week end and overnight camp for Scout troops of the Pikes Peak Region. See Attachment.

The First National Convention of The American Legion convened in Minneapolis and adopted a resolution supporting the Boy Scouts of America as first youth program.

Lord Baden-Powell created Wood Badge training to develop adult leadership and practical scouting skills. The syllabus was a combination of classroom lessons and outdoor skill training, similar to his recommended scout troop program. At the completion of the training, the participant wrote a "ticket", or plan, how to apply the teachings to his scouting position. When the goals were met, two beads (Wood Badge) are awarded to represent the advanced training. Originally the training was over the span of several weeks, but subsequent syllabus adaptations have condensed the material and gradually shortened the training to seven days or two three-day weekends.

On 31 December there were 273 registered Scouts.

1920

A Scout Council was set up in Cripple Creek – Victor region in January of this year.

In January there were 13 active troops and 280 scouters. Thirty-nine boys attended the first period of summer camp held at Camp Vessey in June and 41 boys attended the second period.

On 31 December there were 249 Scouts registered.

1921

As a result of a flood, the road to Camp Vessey was blocked and summer camp had to be moved to Camp Dreamland on the property of Asa Cogswell, a retired dentist, in the Black Forest. Seventy-five boys attended the summer camp.

1922

Raymond J. Davis of Troop 18 (Manitou Springs) was the first scout to receive his Eagle Scout badge*, awarded it 5 March 1922. Raymond attended Colorado College and was closely followed by Clifford Reed, (No. 2) also of Troop 18, who received his Eagle Scout badge on 21 April 1922.

Say "Eagle Scout" and the mind's eye instantly sees a youth who exemplifies being trustworthy, loyal, helpful, friendly, and all those other good things in the Scout Law. Eagle Scouts are such well-known symbol of Scouting's finest that it's hard to believe they haven't always been around. In fact, in the beginning of the Boy Scouts of America, the Eagle Scout Award did not exist. Wolf Scout was the highest award, based on the Silver Wolf award in the advancement plan of Robert S. S. Baden-Powell, the British founder of worldwide Scouting. No Wolf Scout badge was ever given out, though, because the BSA's founding fathers had second thoughts about a wolf as top dog among Scouts. Several leaders who previewed the first proof copies of the 1911 Handbook for Boys asked: "Why a wolf? Why not an American eagle?"

El Paso and Teller Counties Council was the new name for the councils in the Pikes Peak region. They would use that name until 1925.

1923

On 17 February 1923, James E. West* visited Colorado Springs for one day. He was accomplished by Walter W. Head, then Regional President.

James E. West at the White House, with U.S. President Franklin D. Roosevelt and Walter W. Head, BSA national president (seated, left) in 1937

6,000 trees were planted in Waldo Canyon during March and April of that year by Scouts in the area.

Troop 20, sponsored by the Evening Telegraph, won the inter-troop efficiency contest prize of $25 dollars and then donated it to the Community Chest. Troop 23 (First M. E. Church) was second.

The annual summer camp was held at the Skelton Ranch* west of Woodland Park with 75 boys in attendance. The boys kept in touch with home by radio broadcasts sent from the radio station XFUM in The Marksheffel Motor Company building.

* The Skelton Ranch – a dude ranch -- From 1917 to 1940, the resort ranch was largely vacant, although it was used for camping and outings. The Boy Scouts used the abandoned ranch grounds as an encampment in the 1920s. An earlier account of a Boy Scout outing, while the ranch was in operation, was recorded in "Boys Life." After the ranch properties were sold, Judge Skelton and Lizzie moved to Colorado Springs where they practiced their faith (Christian Scientists) in a storefront office in the city. William Skelton died in 1932, followed by Lizzie ten years later. Both are buried in Evergreen Cemetery.

In September 1923 the headquarters report gave the total Scout registration as 404, with 39 Scoutmasters and Assistants registered.

1924

Ralph Hubbard, Scoutmaster of Troop 12, was the third Scouter in the council to receive his Eagle Scout badge on 20 April 1924.

Ralph Hubbard

107 Scouts and 10 adults attended the summer camp, 8 June to 22 June, held at the Skelton Ranch west of Woodland Park.

Colorado Springs Gazette 5/18/1924

"Clear, crisp mornings in the high woodlands and the mystic spell of the council fires are in store for more than 300 Boy Scouts of the Pikes Peak region who will attend the summer encampment at Skelton Ranch, four and a half miles northwest of Woodland Park, between Trout and West creeks, from June 9 to 21 inclusive." What an adventure for local and national Scouts participating in this large event. Ted K Tillitson, Scout Executive stated while talking to the press.

"The Skelton ranch encampment consists of a dozen cabins, scattered over nearly a square mile of rolling country above Woodland Park. Cabins have been found much better from a health standpoint than tents for city boys in the high altitudes".

"The most popular period of the entire day was when the campers gather about a huge fire for discussions and "Stunts." "This is the only period of the day which is not heralded by the bugler. Instead, a lusty-lunged tribesman climbs upon the roof of one of the cabins and gives three long wolf howls -- the council ring call."

Ralph Hubbard and Bernard Hartman, both of Troop 12 sponsored by the Lincoln School, were delegated to attend the annual international Scout Jamboree held in Copenhagen, Denmark. They sailed aboard the Leviathan 24 July. Money to send Hartman ($325) was raised by popular subscription. Hartman won first prize in the first aid contest at the Jamboree.

Robert Liles, Troop 9, sponsored by Cheyenne School, was the fourth scout in the Council to achieve his Eagle Scout badge awarded on 31 August 1924.

In September Scouts collected canned milk for the Near East relief fund. Some 2500 cans were collected. One scout from Troop 19 collected 240 cans of milk for this effort.

James E. West made a brief visit to Colorado Springs on 19 – 20 September after attending the national meeting held in Estes Park, Colorado.

Veldon Long, Troop 12, was the fifth scout to receive the Eagle Scout badge on 5 October 1924.

1925

T. Ernest Nowels, Jr., Troop 8 sponsored by Steele school, earned his Eagle Scout badge 29 March 1925, he was the sixth scout to receive this rank in the Colorado Springs area.

In the first Council Jamboree held at the City Auditorium on 23 May 1925, Troop 2 won first place, followed by Troop 34 in second place and Troop 19 in third place. Nearly 4,000 spectators watched this indoor field meet, with the afternoon devoted to trial events and the finals in the evening.

The annual summer camp was again held at the Skelton Ranch from 8 June to 20 June with 50 boys in attendance.

The El Paso and Teller Counties Council in 1925 changed its name to Pikes Peak Council, which it remains to this day.

"The Growth and Depression Years"

1926 to 1935

1926

Anniversary week was featured by the radio broadcast over station KXFX with our Scout Executive Mr. Barr speaking and a scout quartet singing scout songs.

Campsites within the city were given to scout troops during the spring month. A contest was held to determine the best site and the prize was won by Troop 28 sponsored by the Trinity Methodist Church.

Troop 1 (Stratton Home) won the annual Jamboree followed by Troop 19 and Troop 34 third. A parade through the downtown streets preceded the show.

The council received permission from the city to build a cabin as a headquarters building at the end of Boulder Street abutting up against Monument Valley Park.

The summer camp was held on the Cole Ranch, seven miles north of Woodland Park and three-fourths of a mile west of Camp Colorado. Mr. F.M.P. Taylor donated the equipment which consisted of 10 12X16 tents, 2 6X8 tents, and a cook tent. Sixty-eight boys were in attendance.

Edward H. Mason, Troop 23, was the seventh member of the local Council to be awarded his Eagle Scout badge. The badge was awarded in October of the year. Robert G. Hibbard, Troop 19, was the eighth scout to be awarded his Eagle badge in this Council. He was awarded his badge on 26 November 1926. Robert G. Hibbard was a Distinguished Eagle Scout*.

The Distinguished Eagle Scout Award was established in 1969 to acknowledge Eagle Scouts who have distinguished themselves on a national level, receiving recognition or eminence within their field and who have a strong record of voluntary service to their community. Only Eagle Scouts who earned the Eagle Scout rank a minimum of 25 years previously are eligible for nomination. The award is granted by the National Eagle Scout Association upon the recommendation of a committee of Distinguished Eagle Scouts.

1927

Two more names were added to the Eagle Scout roster when Sam Lairson *(No. 9)* and Joe Kamionka *(No. 10)* members of Troop 1, earned their Eagle rank.

Open house was held at the new headquarters cabin in February. The cabin was 30' by 60' and built of peeled logs. The Council was granted permission by the City Council to build a cabin as a headquarters building at the termination of West Boulder Street, abutting Monument Valley Park. The building was a gift of F. M. P. Taylor.

Charles F. "Chief" Perkins of La Junta was appointed Executive in April and his first task was arranging for the Colorado Wyoming patrol Leaders conference which was held April 22-23 at the First Methodist Church. Eagle Scout Bob Hibbard, Troop 19, was President of the conference and presided at all of the sessions. Over 400 boys attended and they were housed in private homes for the two days.

Alvin Coyle from Troop 30 was awarded his Eagle Scout badge April 4, the eleventh scout in the Council to receive this award.

Donald Haney from Troop 19 was the twelfth scout in the region to win his Eagle Scout badge. Robert Hibbard, Troop 19 was awarded the bronze Eagle Palm on 9 June. (The Eagle Palms was introduced in 1927). An Eagle Scout who earns five merit badges beyond the minimum amount (and meets other requirements) receives a Bronze Palm. A Scout earned a Gold Palm for 10 extra merit badges and a Silver Palm for 15 extra merit badges.

Troop 1, sponsored by the Myron Stratton Home, won the annual field meet held at Washburn Field. Troop 19 placed second and Troop 10 placed third.

Summer camp was held in June and there were 85 Scouts and 7 leaders at camp the second year at Cole's Ranch.

In September, four Eagle Scout badges were awarded at a Court of Honor. Those obtaining the Eagle Scout rank were Charles L. Tutt, Jr.*, from Troop 19, *(No 13)*, James Turner, Troop 19, *(No 14)*, Randolph Riley, Troop 28, *(No 15)*, and James A. Peck, Scoutmaster Troop 19,*(No 16)* .

* Tutt became the secretary of the Broadmoor Hotel and Land Company until Penrose's death in 1939, when he became president of The Broadmoor, owned by Penrose's charitable organization, El Pomar Foundation. He became head of the foundation in 1956 with Julie Penrose's death.

The Tutt Library at Colorado College is named for Tutt, who served as a trustee of Colorado College. In 1959, the house he had lived in with his parents was donated to the school, and it is now known as the Tutt Alumni House. He died in 1961 at the age of 72

Robert Hibbard, Troop 19, was awarded the gold and silver Eagle Palms at the same Court of Honor.

BSA recognition is based on the military model where silver is higher than gold, as in a First Lieutenant with a silver bar outranks a Second Lieutenant with a gold bar.

Hollis Stotesbury from Troop 1 earned his Eagle Scout badge in December, the seventeenth scout to receive this award.

1928

Two more Scouts achieved their Eagle rank when Robert C. Black III, Troop 19, *(No 18)* and John Armstrong, Troop 10, (No. 19) were awarded their Eagle badges at a Court of Honor held March 11th.

Bronze Palms were awarded to Alvin Coyle, Troop 30, and Charles Tutt, Jr., Troop 19. Edward Mason was awarded his fourth combination of Palms representing 56 merit badges. Edward Mason, Troop 23; Jack Fisher, Troop 2: and H. H. Davis, Councilmen were awarded their five year Veteran pins and Frank E. Bumstead his ten year Veteran pin at a Court of Honor held 20 May. Eagle Palms were awarded to Alvin Coyle, Troop 30 and Robert Hibbard, Troop 19.

Harland E. Hedblem, Jr., Troop 2 was awarded his Eagle badge August 12. This was Eagle badge no. 20.

Thirty-two Scouts hiked to Cripple Creek, August 21 to 22, via the Stage Road. "Chief" Perkins, Scout Executive, was in charge of this outing.

Donald Hibbard, Troop 19*, *(No. 21)* and Melvin Williams, Troop 13, *(No. 22)* were awarded their Eagle Scout badges September of this year. George Riley, Troop 23, became the twenty-third scout to achieve the eagle rank in October. Robert Hibbard, Troop 19, received his second combination of Eagle Palms at the same Court of Honor.

* Donald Hibbard was born September 24, 1913 to Cassius A. and Sadie (Vaux) Hibbard. He attended Steele Elementary School, North Junior High School, Colorado Springs High School and graduated from Colorado College in 1935. Donald served in the U.S. Navy during World War II. Donald was a partner in Hibbard and Company Department Store from 1935 until 1950, when his dream called him to the ranching life, raising Black Angus Cattle and alfalfa on his ranch east of Fountain, Colorado. He was greatly pleased when the City of Fountain honored Donald for the donation of part of his ranch by naming a city park after him. Donald was a past member of the Rotary Club of Colorado Springs.

1929

The Pikes Peak Council was incorporated July 17, 1929 and was recorded with the Secretary of State, Denver, Colorado.

Council membership figures showed 507 boys of which 340 were in Colorado Springs; 25 troops; 24 scoutmasters; 28 assistant scoutmasters and 99 troop Committeemen. Summer camp attendance was 80 this year. Scouts gave 4,264 hours of civic service to the community.

On 11 February, 200 Scouts answered a mobilization call at the City Hall to hunt for Frank Auld, Scout with Troop 30, in Austin Bluffs. Later he was found in California where he had hitch-hiked.

The annual Jamboree was held in the City Auditorium on 1 April with 2,000 spectators. David N. Heizer appeared in Civil War uniform and closed the show with his story telling ability.

In May a field meet was held at Prospect Lake with Troop 1 as winners.

Robert Hibbard, Troop 19, was awarded his third combination of Eagle Palms and his five year Veteran badge on 2 June.

Colorado Springs Gazette 5/19/29

"10 Acre Track Near Lake George Theirs: Will Build Summer Camp."

"Thru cooperation of the United States forest service, the Boy Scouts of Colorado Springs and Manitou have come into their own. Theirs to use, and as good as own, is a 10-acre tract of beautiful wooded country six miles north of Lake George 42 miles from Colorado Springs. They will have their summer camp there this year. As soon as school is out, June 7, the boys will start the building of a log cookhouse. Eventually they expect to have a number of log buildings at the place."

Camp Tarryall was dedicated on 13 August this year. *See Attachments. The camp committee was composed of Otis McIntyre, Council President; Russel Law, chairman; E.S. Keithly, Supt Pike National Forest; R. Clifford Black; and Carl S. Chamberlin. "Chief Perkins was the Scout Executive.

A Glider Troop (Troop 6) was organized by Alexander Industries in September with Floyd Engstrom as Scoutmaster.

Velden O. Long, Troop 12, was awarded his ten year Veteran badge; Melvin Williams, Troop 13, was awarded his second combination of Eagle Palms and Bob Hibbard, Troop 19, his fourth combination of Eagle Palms this year. At the same court of Honor William A. Thompson, Scoutmaster of Troop 34 and Estle P. Weaver, Troop 29, Simla CO, were awarded the five year Veteran badge.

The estate of Frank Loud willed 580 acres to the Pikes Peak Council for the development of a Boy Scout camping facility. The property was west of Bear Creek in the area called Jones Park, near Lake Moraine. The homestead land had a two-room cabin and four-room cabin called Chipmunk Lodge. The will stated that the Council must use the land within five years or be forfeited to Frank Loud's heirs. Evidently, Council did not meet the usage requirement. In 1948, the City of Colorado Springs purchased the land from the heirs as part of the city water shed.

One hundred fifty boys used the "Y" (YMCA) pool during that year for swims.

1930

Bernard Vessey (Camp Vessey was named after him) was elected as the Commissioner for the council.

Troop 19 put 400 spruce cones and greeting cards on hospital trays in the city on New Year's Day.

Sam Wultz, Troop 34 was awarded his five year Veteran badge on 3 January.

The fifth Annual Jamboree was held at the City Auditorium on 26 April, with 2,500 people in attendance.

A house warming celebration was held at Camp Tarryall on 14 June when the large cabin was completed.

During June, Troop 18, through the courtesy of the Manitou Kiwanis Club, had a ten day outing to Carlsbad Caverns. Ten Scouts and J. B. Richardson, Scoutmaster, made the trip.

James E. West, Chief Scout Executive of the United States, visited Camp Tarryall on 17 August. Robert Calvert, Troop 32, (No 23) received his Eagle badge at camp from Mr. West. An airmail pouch was dropped by "Red" Mosier* at Camp Tarryall on the same day.

* Mosier was born in Pawnee, OK in 1897 and attended school there, moving later to Austin, TX. His aviation career began with the U.S. Army Signal Corps in 1917. After WWI, he engaged in exhibition flying and barnstorming, semi-professional baseball, and was a high-school football coach. He worked for A.G. Spaulding & Co., the sporting goods manufacturer, until 1927, when he became a test pilot in Colorado Springs, CO. Red Mosier (past vice president of American Airlines) was a test pilot for Alexander Aircraft Company of Colorado Spring, CO.

Camp Tarryall - First Flight Incoming airmail to Camp via Colorado Springs, CO.

Fifty eight boys attended summer camp with 6 leaders. Camp was held at Camp Tarryall.

The Scouts sold Christmas trees at the corner of Kiowa and Nevada for camp funds. Over $160 was realized from the sale.

On December 31 there were 13 Active troops, 12 lapsed or suspended troops, 25 Scoutmasters, 25 assistant Scoutmasters, and 454 boys registered. 144 merit badges were awarded during the year.

1931

Troop 6 built its own glider and regular exhibitions were put on each Sunday afternoon at the Alexander Airport (where the old dog track is located on the east side of Nevada Ave).

Troop 13 planted 1,800 tree seedlings at Camp Tarryall under the direction of the U.S. Forest Service.

A field meet was held on 6 June at the corner of Platte and Cascade Avenues. Troop 13 was first; Troop 10 second and Troop 2 third.

A Gold Eagle Palm was awarded to Floyd Engstrom, Scoutmaster of Troop 6 on 28 June, and Bob Glow, Troop 10, was awarded his five year Veteran badge. Robert Hibbard, Troop 19 was awarded his fifth combination of Eagle Palms and Floyd Engstrom, Troop 6, his first combination of Eagle Palms.

During the year the Council celebrated its Fifteenth Anniversary having a total registration of 24 troops and 653 boys.

In August, 50,000 rainbow trout fingerlings were planted in the Platte and Tarryall rivers.

The total membership record for the year was 687 with 462 new boys registered, 20 active troops, no lapsed or suspended troops, 20 Scoutmasters and 22 Assistant Scoutmasters.

Sixty two boys attended summer camp with 9 leaders. Two hundred boys spent week-ends at camp during the year. Troop 18 from Manitou, spent ten days on the Western Slope of Colorado with ten boys in the party.

145 tenderfoot, 78 second class, 28 first class, 28 star awards, and 463 merit badges were granted during the year. 2,446 hours of civic service were given. $500 worth of improvements was added at Camp Tarryall.

1931 First Silver Beaver awards presented by local councils. The Silver Beaver award was created by the National Council and first presented in 1931 as an award program to be utilized by a local council with National Council approval of the recipients. The first year they were presented nationally (1931), they were on a pocket ribbon like an Eagle Scout medal. After that first year they were placed on neck ribbons and remain so to this day.

Silver Beaver awards were presented to Dr. S. W. Schaeffer and Lester Griswold, Council members, at the annual meeting held in December. Dr. S. W. Schaeffer was reelected national delegate to BSA.

1932

Lloyd Weide, Troop 2 was awarded his Eagle badge on 15 January, the twenty-fifth scout in the Council to have won this award.

Gunnar Berg, National Director of Volunteer Training, spoke here on 4 February.

The sixth annual Jamboree was held 6, 7 May at the City Auditorium with 2,000 people as guests.

In April, Eagle badges were awarded to Conrad Brown, Troop 18; Richard Bloss, Troop 18, and Carrel Bullock, Troop 10, Jimmie Millward, Troop 2, and Everard Woodsoon, Troop 13.

Professor Gordon Parker officially represented the Pikes Peak Council at the National Council meeting held in New York City in May.

During July, 71 boys were in camp during a ten day period.

The Silver Beaver award was presented to Scoutmaster William A Thompson, Troop 34, at the annual meeting.

The twenty year Veteran pin was awarded to Lester Griswold*, and Eagle badges were given to Howard Brooks, Troop 10; Bob Glow, Assistant Scoutmaster, Troop 10; Arnold Steele, Troop 2; and Bert Reuler, Troop 10 in October this year.

Lester Griswold was a Scout Leader of Troop 10 in Colorado Springs. In addition, Griswold was an author of nine different versions of a handicraft book and put together a program of Native American Dancing for the troop's project.

Bronze Palms awards were earned by Richard Bless, Troop 18; Conrad Brown, Troop 18; and Carroll Bullock, Troop 10 at a Court of Honor held in Perkins Hall.

National Bank Building

The scout office was located in Room 215, Colorado Springs National Bank Building from January to September and then moved to a room in the Chamber of Commerce.

1932 saw five year Veteran badge awarded to Melvin Williams, Scoutmaster, Troop 2; Eugene Essick, Scoutmaster, Troop 13; Willis E Armstrong, Troop 19; Robert Black, III, Troop 19; and Charles L. Tutt, Jr., Troop 19. Eagle badges were presented to Frank Auld, Scoutmaster, Troop 30 and Bob Burns, Troop 19.

484 Scouts were registered in December of this year.

1933

Twenty Scouts under the leadership of Scout Executive C. F. Perkins and Eugene Essick attended the World's Fair in Chicago during August.

"Chief" Perkins resigned in August and Willard R. Olsen, formerly Assistant Executive at Davenport Iowa, was appointed to succeed him as Scout Executive.

Forty-nine Scouts and five leaders attended summer camp.

A Cub Committee of the Council was organized in the fall and six requests were received for Cub Packs.

In December a new road was built to Camp Vessey from the Bear Creek Canyon road through C. W. A.* funds.

*The Civil Works Administration was created on November 9, 1933. It was intended to be a short term program designed to carry the nation over a critical winter while other programs such as the Federal Emergency Relief Administration were being planned and developed. Its original aim was to put 4 million needy unemployed to work for the winter of 1933-1934. CWA projects were sponsored primarily by local state governments, and every attempt was made to fit the projects to the local people in need of work.

270 merit badges were awarded during the year.

During the spring and summer months very little scouting was done in this area and registration rolls dropped to some 260 boys.

1934

The first "Lone Scout" unit* was registered in the Council at Woodland Park, Troop 25, in January.

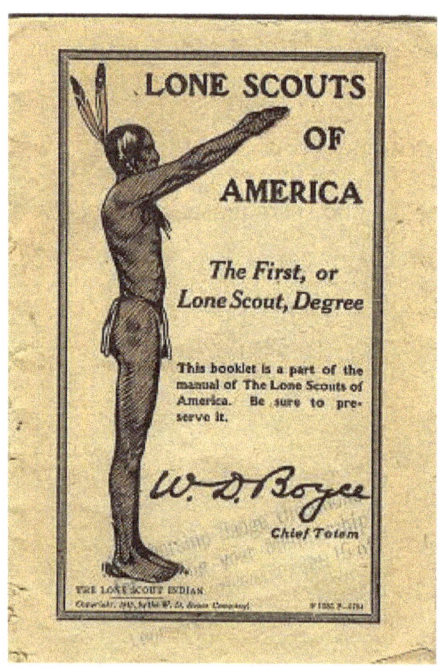

* Lone Scouts have been around since William D. Boyce organized the Lone Scout of America (LSA) in 1915. Boyce had noticed that rural boys were being left out of Scouting because they did not live near a town or could not travel to a Scout Troop in the nearest town. As a "Lone Scout", a boy he thought could enjoy Scouting. His Lone Scouts would have a different set of requirements they could meet on their own, leading to various "degrees" (the "degree" concept was probably based upon the Masonic rite's various

degrees, as Boyce was also a Mason). Because of Boyce's journalistic background, Lone Scouts had a strong program of writing and correspondence. W. D. Boyce was the "Chief Totem" – the administrator – of the Lone Scouts of America. He bankrolled the Lone Scouts from his own newspaper companies. Lone Cub Scouting and Lone Scouting still exist today, as official program options of the Boy Scouts of America, but there are only a few hundred members now.

In the National Old Clothing Drive in February by Scouts throughout the United States, local Scouts did their share, collecting several truckloads of clothing and household furnishings.

Forty-nine Scouts under the direction of Bob Hibbard, Scoutmaster, Troop 23, visited the C. F. and I. Company steel plant in Pueblo in March.

The Scout Executive moved his home into the cabin on Boulder Street. During March the scout office was moved from the Chamber of Commerce to Room 18 in the Independence Building*.

*The structure was renamed the Independence Building in 1910 in honor of Stratton's flagship Independence Mine, discovered on the Fourth of July 1891. Operated by the Stratton estate, the profits from the building benefited the Myron Stratton Home, an institution created through Stratton's will to provide for poor children and the elderly on an estate on Nevada Avenue, south of downtown.

The troop commissioner idea was finally perfected and the Council was divided into four districts with a district commissioner at the head of each district. District 1 included troops 3,5,18, and 24 with O. J. Miller as Commissioner; District 2 included troops 1, 8, 19, 23 and 34 with Dr. Beryl Ritchey Commissioner; District 3 included troops 2, 10 and 30 with Ted Thomas Commissioner; and District 4 included troops 4, 7 and 13 with Kenneth Tolley Commissioner. Herbert Stockdale was appointed Cub Commissioner.

During the year, 1,367 Scouts gave 3,865 hours of civic service which included ushering at the College football and basketball games; ushering at the civic concerts; collecting boxes for the Chamber of Commerce; horse and pony show; Christian endeavor conference; Chamber of Commerce banquet; Townsend pension meetings; pages for Rotary convention; Disabled American Veterans convention; delivered folders for the Community Chest; delivering Christmas baskets to poor families; delivering C. W. A. job notices; Straw Hat day parade; Fourth of July parade; Indian dancing for the tourists; Paint-up week; and Greeters Day.

Advancement records during the year showed 113 boys passing the Second Class rank; 35 Scouts passing the First Class requirements; 9 Scouts passing the Star Scout requirements; and 2 Scouts completing the Life Scout requirements. 210 merit badges in 42 different subjects were awarded. 78 of these merit badges or 37% were earned by Troop 23 of the First Methodist Church.

Final records showed 563 Scouts, 15 Sea Scouts, 125 Cub Scouts, and 230 adult scouters registered as of December 31. Of the total number of Scouts registered, 240 had been Scouts less than one year; 186 less than two years; 90 less than three years; 41 less than four years; 17 less than five years; and 9 over five years.   Three elementary training courses, Part 1, were given with 34 scouters completing the full requirements.

1934 -- The Order of the Arrow becomes an approved part of the Scouting program.

1935

The annual meeting was held at the Acacia Hotel*, 15 January, with Robert W. Kelso*, State Relief Director, and former member of the National Boy Scout Council, the principal speaker.

Robert Kelso earned his A.B. in 1904 and his LL.B. in 1907, both at Harvard. He practiced law from 1907 to 1910. He was an instructor, lecturer, or honorary lecturer at several institutions, including Harvard College, Simmons College School of Social Work, and Washington University's George Warren Brown School of Social Work. He held several positions in social service agencies, including secretary of the Massachusetts State Board of Charities; commissioner of Public Welfare, State of Massachusetts; secretary of the Boston Council of Social Agencies; director, St. Louis Community Fund and Council; director Federal Emergency Relief Service, Colorado State Relief Administration. He was president of the National Conference of Social Work in 1922.

The Acacia Park Hotel opened on July 7, 1907 to cater to tourists and business travelers visiting the Pike Peak region. When a fourth story was added in 1910, the 150-room building was called "one of few stylish hotels" in Colorado Springs.

The Pampa News, Texas, reported that thirty-six Boy Scouts and 11 men left in high spirits for Camp Tarryall at Lake George Colorado, where they were to work and play for 10 days.

Colorado Gazette and Telegraph June 16, 1935 "Boy Scouts Go to Tarryall Today"

"...Boy Scouts will set the fashion for this summer sport, for their Camp Tarryall, near Lake George is the first to open. A party of 10 boys will be there today and it is expected no less than 100 will make stays at the camp during the four weeks that it will be open. ...On July 1 the camp will reopen for parties of boys of about 40 in a group, which will be sent weekly by the *Omaha World-Herald*. They will pass about four days of the week there."

Something happened to Camp Tarryall after this date but we could not find any evidence. It was reported that a flood destroyed the camp and we also heard there was a change in the leadership of the Pike National Forest and they did not want permanent buildings on Park grounds so denied their rebuilding efforts. Camp Tarryall has been lost to history.

"The War Years"
1936 to 1945

1936

Boy Scouts parade down Tejon Street, followed by men on horseback wearing cowboy clothing

1936 First Wood Badge courses held in USA following English syllabus.

1937

1937 1st National Jamboree, Washington, DC attendance 27,232

The first National Jamboree was to be held in Washington, D.C. in 1935 but was canceled due to the polio epidemic. In 1937, the Jamboree that these nine Koshares Indian dancers traveled to became the first National Jamboree. Ralph Hubbard helped escort these Koshares dancers to Washington, D.C. During the Jamboree they worked with Carl Parlasca and his Big Timber Dancers from Elgin, IL. The Jamboree was held on the site of what is now the Lady Byrd Johnson Memorial Park.

1938

Waite Phillips donates Philturn Rocky Mountain Scout camp (later to become Philmont Scout Ranch) consisting of 35,857 acres of land on the eastern slope of the Rocky Mountains, near Cimarron, New Mexico.

1939

1939 Philturn Rocky Mountain Scout camp opens, Air Scouting added.

1940

More than 2,500 persons crowded into the municipal auditorium, filled the boxes on the lower floor, jammed the balconies and overflowed the hallways to watch one of the most successful Boy Scout, Sea Scout and Cub Circuses ever staged here in Colorado Springs. The 1940 edition not only proved a six-ring circus furnished fun and frolic for all, but also showed the educational and character-building features of the movement. About 500 Scouts participated in this event.

Historic 1940s Scout Lodges now on the USAF Academy

Activities during the year were the Scout Circus and 14 different civil projects.

At years end, there were 24 troops, with 466 boys and 4 packs with 292 Cubs. There were 135 adult scouters and 18 adult scouters for Cub Scouts.

1941

1941 Webelos rank created in Cub Scouting; Philturn renamed Philmont Scout Ranch, and Lord Baden-Powell passes away.

With the declaration of war, the government requests Boy Scout service for the distribution of defense bonds and stamp posters; collection of aluminum and wastepaper; defense housing surveys; victory gardens; distribution of air-raid posters; cooperation with the American Red Cross; and, by joint agreement with the Office of Civil and Defense Mobilization, services in three capacities--messengers, assisting emergency medical units, and firewatchers.

Waite Phillips makes another large gift--land, residence and ranch buildings, livestock, operating ranch equipment--contiguous to Philturn Rocky Mountain Scout camp, bringing total acreage to more than 127,000 acres. The area is renamed Philmont Scout Ranch.

Webelo rank created for 11-year-old boys with the Lion badge.

Summer camp on council site was attended by 4 troops (71 Scouts) and held in 10 mile canyon. The Camporee was attended by 80 Scouts. A mobilization was held on 15 November in the Garden of the Gods and was an outstanding success.

At the end of the year there were 26 troops with 487 Scouts and 7 packs with 254 Cubs. There were 156 adult scouters and 68 adults in Cub Scouts.

1942

Scouts continue in war service. Twenty-eight projects are requested by the government, including the collection of 30 million pounds of rubber in a two-week drive; all-out salvage based on the government-issued pamphlet Scrap and How Scouts Collect It; distribution of pledge cards for war bonds and savings stamps; victory gardens; work on farms and in harvest camps; and government dispatch bearers.

Lt Peterson, an Eagle Scout, died in an aircraft accident at Colorado Springs Army Air base in August this year and in December the base was named after him, Peterson Field.

Some activities throughout the year were Distributing Community Chest folders and distributing War Bond and Stamp posters to Colorado Springs business firms. Tree planting in the Pike National Forest was conducted where 47 Scouts worked 4 weeks in a regular tree planting camp under professional supervision. An estimated 225 tons of scrap rubber was collected in a Council wide effort. 18 Scouts worked 3 hours each picking up nails at Peterson Field for the U. S. Government as they built the new Colorado Springs Army Air Corps base. The Scouts assisted the police for the 4th of July parade and worked as messengers in Civil Defense projects. In summary more than 50,000 hours of service was rendered by the Scouts of the Pikes Peak Council supporting the war effort.

Columbia School Cub Scout Pack received an Indian tee pee to commemorate the Indian Chief Aquila. His teachings are what the Cub packs follow.

At year's end there were 32 troops with 609 Scouts; 11 Sea Scouts; 20 Explorers, 8 Air Scouts; 2 lone Scouts and 202 adult Scouters. There were 9 Cub packs with 250 Cubs; 93 adult Cub Scouts, 33 Den mothers and 33 Den Chiefs.

1943

Scouts were involved in salvaging 20 tons of waste paper and scrap metal with 600 Scouts participating; distributing Government posters and "Keep 'Em Flying" posters.

Total Scouts for the year was 30 Troops with 584 Scouts; 11 Sea Scouts; 28 Explorers: 27 Air Scouts; 11 Senior Scouts; and 4 Lone Scouts. There were 14 Cub Packs with 375 Cubs; 109 adult Cub Scouts; 46 Den mothers and 46 Den Chiefs in the Council.

1944

Area Scouts continued with their War time services by collecting over 10,000 lbs. of waste paper supporting the war effort. They also distributed 10,000 Government Circulars and Government Informational Material. Over 75 Scouts in 15 Troops supported the Government War Bond Drive. Even with the war going on, 17 Troops with 255 Scout and 27 Scouters attended long term camping on the Council Camp Site.

The Scout Service Center moves to Carlton Building room 305.

Membership for the year was 28 Troops with 587 Scouts; 7 Explorers; 21 Air Scouts; 27 Sea Scouts; 11 Senior Scouts and 5 Lone Scouts. There were 17 Packs with 579 Cubs; 151 adult Cub Scouts; 54 Den Mothers; and 46 Den Chiefs.

1945

Council summer camp totals were 20 Troops with 251 Scouts and 30 Scouters held in Camp Ewing*. Camp Ewing has been used as a bible camp and conference center, Colorado College's geological camp, U.S. Forest Service area and is still being used by various groups. It is now called Camp Elim.

Ewing, Earl: established Camp Ewing across road from Camp Colorado and eventually this was also given to Colorado College.

A Camporee was held in Black Canyon* and was attended by 275 Scouts.

The only information found was Black Canyon is near Manitou Springs off Highway 24.

Camp Vessey was used 35 weekends by the Scouts and a new roof was installed in September of this year.

Again the Council Scouts collected waste paper (60,000 lbs.); distributed Circulars (12,000); Government Information Materials (3,000) and War Fund Drive Circulars (25,000). 36 units provided window displays for anniversary week and most all units participated in Sunday Church services during that week.

The total number of Scouts at year end was 28 Troops with 716 Scouts and there were 17 Packs with 750 Cubs; 156 adult Cub Scouts; 64 Den Bothers; 50 Den Chiefs. During the year 79 Cubs became 12 years of age and 59 became Scouts.

"Renew and Regrowth Years"

1946 to 1955

1946

Camp Alexander was purchased in January for $25,832.22 for camp property. The camp was named after Don M. Alexander, Council President who has provided much personal effort and large sums of money to develop the camp.")

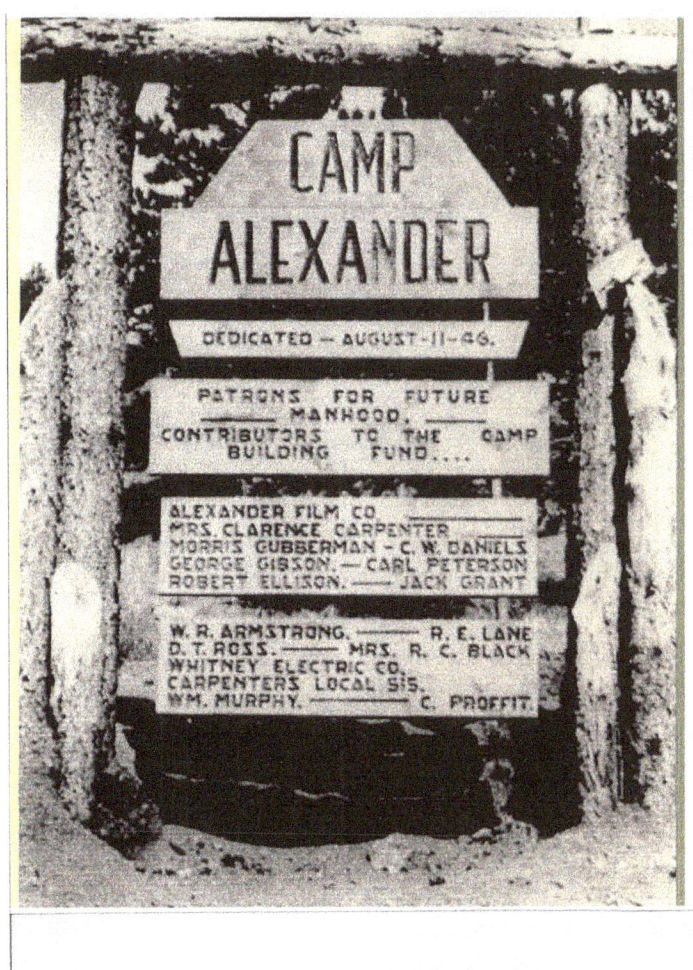

125 adults attended Cub Leaders' Pow Wow in Colorado Springs this year.

A special committee was selected by the Executive Board in January 1944 to serve as a Camp Development Committee. The members were, Don M Alexander, Lester Griswold, Lester Howard, Guy McDowell, George Gibson, Matt Whitney, Paul McCord and Walter Peterson.

Camp Alexander 1946

A very attractive camp site was finally selected in Eleven Mile Canyon which consisted of 370 acres of land completely surrounded by the Pike National Forest. After much study and planning by the Camp Development Committee and National Headquarters Engineers a long term program of building and development was completed. In the planning stages the site was called Rankin's Gulch. At the dedication Ceremonies in August the camp was officially named "Camp Alexander".

44 Scouts attended the first camp at Camp Alexander in August after the dedication.

Total Scout troops this year were 32 which included 1 Air Scout; 1 Sea Scout; 1 Explorer and 1 "Negro" African- American Scout troop (10 boys). There were 672 Scouts and 406 Scouters. There were 830 Cub Scouts with 203 adult Cub Scouts.

1947

Over 400 Scouts and Leaders attended the June camporee at Camp Alexander. Camp Vessey was used by many troops for day and overnight hikes.

The Scout Circus sponsored by the Colorado Springs Junior Chamber of Commerce was held with more than 8,500 tickets sold for a new profit of $3,350.

Other activities included distribution of posters, collection of food and clothing, contributions to Santa Claus Shop, campaigns for European relief and ushering at football games.

This year saw 37 Troops with 755 boys and 277 adult Scouters assisting them; 4 senior Scouts with 53 young men and 31 adults. There were 26 Packs with 940 boys plus 269 adult Cub Scouts helping them.

1948

The Council held a Camporee and 525 boys attended.

Enrollment this year was 38 troops with 790 Boy Scouts; 76 Senior Scouts; 28 Packs with 967 Cub Scouts; 310 adult Cub Scouts and 313 adult Scouters. During the year 190 Cubs became age 12 and 139 became Scouts.

1949

Top Scouts Circus Ticket Salesmen of 1949 --- Do you recognize some of these handsome "sharp appearing" Scouts? They were the outstanding ticket salesmen for the 1949 Scout Circus. Many of them have become outstanding business and professional leaders of Colorado Springs and other communities. Left to right are Carl Peterson, Joseph Smith, Anthony Benforte, Robert Phelps (Chairman of the Jaycee Circus Committee), Jerry Seldi, Robert Spear, Tom Stone and Harold Flynn. Most of these men are Scout leaders today. Photo from Gazette news paper

July 1949, More than 600 boys and their leaders spent one to four weeks at the Boy Scouts' Camp Alexander in the summer of 1949. Scout Executive Ray M. Ryerson shows Scout Clyde Mack an ox yoke shipped from New Hampshire by Lester Griswold – in the background is the Clarence Carpenter Memorial Handicraft lodge.

July 1949 – Camp Alexander's new first aid station, gift of Colorado Springs' Lions club.

Frank Perkins Kiva at Camp Alexander

Pride and joy of Pikes Peak Council Boy Scouts is a brand new $25,000 dining hall at Camp Alexander, in Eleven-Mile Canyon. The rustic style, two story structure has been built for the Scouts by EPO Elks Lodge 309 and will be ready for use when camp opens in July. The Handicraft Lodge was built in 1946 as a memorial to Clarence Carpenter, second president of the Pikes Peak Council. It is believed to be one of the best equipped Boy Scout handicraft lodges in the nation according to Ray M. Ryerson, Scout Executive. The lodge is equipped with $6,000 worth of tools for working with leather, wood or metal. This location is now the Wooten Center.

Enrollment this year ended with 984 Scouts; 92 Explorers and 92 adults. Cubs had 1305 Cubs; 440 adult Cub Scouts and 419 adults supporting Scouts. 450 boys attended the Council Camporee this year.

1950

February 1950 – " A huge program of activities in celebration of the 40th anniversary of Scouting is in store for the 2,400 Cub Scouts, Boy Scouts and Explorer Scouts of the Pikes Peak Region", according to Ray Ryerson, Scout executive.

Hundreds of articles of handicraft, hobbies, and merit badges will be displayed by the 80 troops and packs in prominent windows throughout the Pikes Peak council. All window displays will be in place by February.

Official Boy Scout Church day will be observed first Sunday in February with hundreds of Cubs, Scouts and leaders throughout the six and a half counties in the Pikes Peak Council.

The Tri-district Court of Honor will coincide with the dedication of the Statue of Liberty. The Court of Honor will be held at City Auditorium immediately following the dedication ceremony.

Statue of Liberty   (Photo 2012)

With the faith and courage of their forefathers who make possible the freedom of these United States

The Boy Scouts of America

Dedicate this replica of the statue of Liberty as a pledge everlasting fidelity and loyalty

40th anniversary crusade to strengthen the arm of liberty

One of the main features of Anniversary week would be the Civic Day celebration when one representative of each Boy Scout troop will occupy a city or county office.

2nd National Jamboree, Valley Forge, PA attendance 47,163.

66 Springs Scouts to Attend Jamboree at Valley Forge, PA. A quota of 66 boys from the Pikes Peak Council of Boy Scouts of America will be allowed to attend the National Jamboree to be held June 30 through 8 July in Valley Forge, PA.

The cost of the entire 3 week trip has been tentatively set at $225, including all transportation, food, tentage, side trips, insurance and some spending money.

"Valley Forge, Pa, President Truman stood up before nearly 50,000 Boy Scouts last night and told them man-to-man what a tough world they are growing up in. It will be an even worse world, the president said, unless all Americans work for peace and freedom with the same burning faith that inspired the men of George Washington's army here at Valley Forge".

Cub Scouts enter 20 floats in Peak Rodeo Parade. This will be the first year Cub Scouts as a group has participated and also the first time so many local youths – 500 in the Scout section alone – have ridden in the parade. The theme of the event was "The Heritage of the West."

Scout Service Center moves to Alta Vista Hotel.

By that year, there were 1,234 Cub Scouts, 934 Boy Scouts and 113 Senior Scouts in the Pikes Peak Council.

1951

70% of the units had an effective camping program.

One of the special events this year was the tree planting with Isaac Walton League.

At the end of 1951 there were 3,494 individuals enrolled in the BSA program. Of that number there were 52 Troops, 36 Packs, 9 Explorer units. The total boys broke out as 1,014 Scouts; 1,366 Cubs Scouts; 115 Explorers; 544 adult Cub Scouts; 148 adult Scouters; 57 adult Explorers; and 250 adults in the scouting program.

1952

Activities this year included a camporee at Camp Alexander; Scout-O-Rama in Colorado Springs and Burlington; Civic Day in Colorado Springs; Explorer Expeditions; Cub Hobby Shows' and Philmont Scout Ranch for 20 Explorers and 5 Scouters.

That year ended with 4,140 total registered with the Council. That was made up of 55 Troops, 39 Packs and 10 Explorer Posts. There were 2,686 boys and 1,454 adults registered.

1953

1953 3rd National Jamboree, Irving Ranch, CA attendance 45,401.

This is the first year that "Friends of Scouting" (FOS) was listed as income for the Council.

350 boys were taught to swim 50 feet with 270 boys passing the standard Scout Camp Swimmers test of 100 yards. 20 Scouts were presented the Lifeguard Award.

4,194 was the total enrolled with BSA at the end of 1953. 55 Troops, 44 Packs, 6 Explorer posts made up of 1,058 Scouters; 1,563 Cubs; 81 Explorers with the adults totaling 577 Scouts; 631 adult Cub Scouts and 38 adult Explorers with 246 other members.

1954

Jim Bates – AdAmAn Photographer and Historian. In 1954 he was one of the leaders of a three day Pikes Peak hike for Explorer Scouts. After hiking up North Cheyenne Canyon and across the saddle to Bear Creek, the Scouts camped in Jones Park where they dined on Army rations. On the second day they passed Lake Moraine, bushwhacked to Barr Trail, and camped at timberline in and around Fred Barr's original timberline shelter cabin. Then, on Labor Day they climbed the peak and watched the Pikes Peak Hill Climb. At least one of the Scouts remembers having considered Jim Bates as the ideal leader for his first climb of a 14,000 foot peak.

The income from Scout-O-Rama was budgeted for improvements at Camp Alexander, assistance for needy boys to attend camp, advancement badges and Explorer Conference. Improvements to Camp Alexander that year included New Adirondack Lean-tos, new latrines, oiling buildings, additional tents, additional Skell gas, new parking area and re-vamped water lines.

The second annual Explorer Conference was held at the Broadmoor Hotel with 305 Explorers attending from 6 different councils.

Long term camping was attended by 37 units, 631 boys and 55 adults at Camp Alexander.

The year-end totals for Scouts were 42 Packs, 52 Troops and 8 Explorer posts with 1,572 Cubs, 1,145 Boy Scouts and 124 Explorers. There were 598 adult Cub Scouts, 463 adult Scouters, 52 Explorer adults and 298 other adults, for a total of 4,252 members.

1955

In 1955 100,000 chartered units were reached nationally.

The most successful civic service event during the year was the Scouts helping with the Pikes Peak Hill Climb Service.

There were 4,815 boys and adults listed with the Council this year with 45 Packs, 54 Troops, and 9 Explorers, 1,903 Cubs, 1,208 Boy Scouts and 154 Explorers in the units. There were 1,550 adults helping out their boys in the Council.

"The Expansion Years"

1956 to 1965

1956

Long term camping saw 490 boys attending on Council site (Camp Alexander) and 299 boys attending sites out of Council locations. 75% of the units camped at least 10 days and nights during the year.

Over 20,000 people attended the Circuses, Camporee, Roundup and Scout Week held by council and districts throughout the year. Over 9,000 boys attended these events also.

"These six Cub Scouts from Pack 10 of Steele School will be among those appearing in a covered wagon scene, one of the highlights in the Scout Circus. The cubs (from left) are Dick Kennedy, Bill Snyder, Jim Kennedy, John Sampson, Shugrue and Charles Stone. The cubs will present "The Story of the Pikes Peak Region." Photo appeared in the Colorado Springs Gazette Telegraph on 18 March

1956 ended with a grand total of 5,395 boys and adults registered in the Council. This was made up of 48 Cub units with 2,195 boys, 59 Scout troops with 1,107 boys and 12 Explorer units with 387 young adults. Camping on site were 43 units with 490 boys and 41 adults Scouters in attendance.

1957

4th National Jamboree, Valley Forge, PA attendance 50,100

Funds ($25,000) were taken from the trust fund to provide a swimming pool for Camp Alexander this year.

Year-end organizations were 49 Cub units with 2,444 boys, 59 Boy Scouts with 1,137 boys, and 13 Explorer units with 441 young adults. There were 1,689 adults assisting in the Scouting program this year.

1958

25 Scouts assisted in fighting a forest fire near the Camp Alexander facility.

Activities through-out the year included Boy Scout Week, Circuses, Fair Participation, Roundup, Civic Day, "Citizens Now" Conference and Explorer Ball.

The year ended with 54 Cub units and 2,730 boys, 59 Boy Scout troops with 1,238 boys and 14 Explorer units with 395 young adults. There were 1,573 adults assisting in the Scouting program this year. Camping showed 801 boys and 68 adults camping on Council site.

1959

In December, 1959, two Explorer Scouts in Pikes Peak Council were selected to join the honor of the annual New Year's Hill Climb. Explorer Scouts, Jeffery Davis and Don Ellis, were selected to be guests of the AdAmAn Club for the New Year's Eve climb to Pikes Peak.

The Explorer Scouts lit the first flares on the top of Pikes Peak at 11:50 as a prelude to the regular fireworks display which is the normal procedure of the AdAmAn Club's New Year's Celebration.

The two Explorers were selected from 20 of the top Explorers in the Pikes Peak region. Each Explorer Post submitted its outstanding mountain climber as a candidate. The club extended the invitation in cooperation with the 50th Anniversary of the Boy Scouts of America, and as an official invitation to the Scouts of America to attend the 5th National Jamboree held in Colorado Springs in 1960.

Of an anecdotal note, the first Explorer Scout, Don Ellis, made the climb again on his 50th anniversary of the first Scout New Year's hill climb.

Activities performed through-out the year were Boy Scout Week observance, Launched 50th Anniversary, Explorer "Citizen Now" Conference, Camporees, Circus, Expeditions, and Webelos Day at Camp Alexander.

Camp Alexander held the following projects; First Aid-O-Ree, Swimming Instruction classes, Marksmanship Matches, Fire Protection Training at camp.

The year ended with 55 Cub units with 2,113 boys, 58 Boy Scout troops with 1,567 boys and 16 Explorer posts with 196 young adults. There were 1,570 adults assisting with the Scouting program.

1960

5th National Jamboree, Colorado Springs, CO attendance 53,378

From July 22 to 29, 1960 the Reverse Diamond J Ranch north of Colorado Springs was the fourth-largest city in Colorado, as 55,000 Scouts and thousands more adults converged for the 5th National Boy Scout Jamboree. For seven days, the boys earned merit badges, attended ceremonies and rodeos, explored the mountains and traded patches, trinkets, cultures.

Boy Scout Jamboree members Dr. Arthur A. Schuch, Chief Scout Executive; Dr. Charles Hiestand, Director of National Jamboree; with Girls of the West from Pikes Peak or Bust Rodeo.

Colorado Springs was the scene of the Fifth National Boy Scout Jamboree. The Boy Scouts movement was founded in England in 1907 by Lord Robert Baden-Powell, and on 08 February 1910 the Boy Scouts of America were founded in Washington, DC. By 1960 there were more than five million American Boy Scouts, and by today more than thirty million Americans have been members of the Scout movement.

Given this fifty-year jubilee, the organization planned a large festivity, which Lord Baden Powell, the son of the founder, would personally attend. Delegations of Boy Scouts were invited from all over the world.

Historic photo taken of the Official Entrance to the Jamboree Camp

This Jamboree was to be the largest Boy Scout Camp ever held in the United States, and the entire event was therefore simply one series of superlatives! The organization was enormous, every detail was checked and rechecked, and nothing was left to chance.

A suitable campsite was found some eight miles north of Colorado Springs, next to the 14,110 ft. high Pikes Peak. The enormous surface of some four square miles was obligingly made available by the Reverse J Diamond Ranch.

It took two years of preparation with hundreds of volunteers to transform this vast area into a tent city called Jamboree City, which actually temporarily became the fourth largest city in Colorado! There was a large arena, roads, water mains, electrical cables, a postal service, a bank, a newspaper (90,000 papers per day!), a 60-acre field hospital, and several stores called Trading Posts.

Extensive contacts were made with suppliers, the railroads, the U.S. Army and Navy, and legions of volunteers. The huge project attracted many donations from generous benefactors. The entire Jamboree ended up being financed entirely through donations and a contribution of fifty dollars from every participating Boy Scout!

Seventy-two thousand people were present at the opening ceremony, including 650 Scouts from 26 other countries. Next to the 56,377 participating Boy Scouts, there were more than 200,000 visitors! During the ceremony the Navy's Flight Demonstration Team, the Blue Angels, flew over the entire campsite and gave a 20-minute demonstration with four jet airplanes.

It took incredible logistics to feed all these Boy Scouts. The volume of food and accessories that was brought in per train was awesome: 2,800 tons or 97 train wagons! Every day 21,000 loaves of bread and 2,183 gallons of milk were distributed, and 16,380 open charcoal fires were burning at the same time. More than 1,278,000 meals were prepared during the event and in one week more than 9.5 million paper plates, cups and other objects were used...

During the Jamboree there was no lack of things to do. There was a full-fledged rodeo by the local Pikes Peak or Bust Rodeo crew, with bull riding, bull dogging, saddle bronco riding, calf roping and bareback riding. There were three large Skill-O-Rama areas, where the Scouts could exhibit their talents as cook or rope maker, and there were all kinds of folklore.

Many foreign Boy Scouts also showed their talents, and there was fire making and several local Indian dances. The Scouts exchanged all kinds of objects such as badges, neckerchiefs and sliders, knives, woodwork, beadwork, leather objects, ceramics and swords.

A few amusing anecdotes managed to escape the mists of time. One scouter remembers spending the first night sleeping on a table, as our tents and beds hadn't arrived yet... Smoking was of course prohibited, but there was one special circumstance where a cigarette was allowed: when you got bitten by a tick!

This bothersome insect nestles itself under the skin and is nearly impossible to dislodge. The American solution is most practical; light a cigarette and burn the insect right through the skin! After that you were allowed to smoke the rest of the cigarette, to soothe your nerves...

President "Ike" Eisenhower honored the event with his presence and drove through the entire camp, widely acclaimed by all. It was estimated that more than 100.000 pictures were taken!

President Eisenhower with Boy Scouts at the 1960 National Jamboree

HOW DO YOU MEASURE HAPPINESS—Terry Schmidt, 16, a student at Cheyenne Mountain School, sits in the cockpit of an Air Force Jet as a representative of five Air Explorer Scouts from Squadron 1 sponsored by the Air Defense Command. Watching his extremely obvious delight are Col. Howard H. Claud Jr., assistant chief of staff for Hq., ADC, and chairman of the Ent AFB scouting committee, and Capt. Robert E. Gregory, instructor pilot. Son of Mr. and Mrs. Kenneth Schmidt, young Schmidt began his scouting career as a Cub Scout and has advanced through the program to the highly specialized Air Explorers.
(Air Force Photo)

Camping on Council site was 55 units with 1,200 Scouts and 98 adults this year.

Membership at year-end was 58 Cub Scout units with 3,086 boys, 62 Troops with 1,732 boys and 15 Explorer Posts with 254 young adults. There were 1,651 adults assisting the scouting program.

1961

Activities through-out the year were: Scout Week, Camporee, Merit Badge Show, Explorer Expeditions, and Conservation Projects at Camp and Annual New Year's Eve climb of Pikes Peak.

Membership at year-end was 57 Cub units with 3,106 boys, 64 Boy Scout troops with 1,398 boys, 17 Explorer posts with 306 young adults. There were 1,728 adults assisting in the Scouting program. 50 troops with 978 boys and 90 troop leaders attended a Council Camp site.

1962

Boy Scout Center dedicated – The Boy Scout Service Center, 522 E. Uintah St., was dedicated at a ceremony beginning at 3 o'clock. The land was purchased from the City of Colorado Springs, and is 480 feet long by 140 feet deep. The building was designed by Bunts and Kelsey architects with advice from the National Council, Boy Scouts of America engineering services.

The building includes 4,400 square feet of floor space and provides offices for four Scout Executives, receptionist, clerical office, duplication and mailing room, program development room, multipurpose room for committee meetings and Scouters training, a small conference room, kitchen and display areas.

The building is especially designed to provide every possible assistance to the 2,500 adult Scouters, who will serve more than 7,000 Cub Scouts, Boy Scouts and Explorers during the current year.

The total cost of the land, construction of the building, all interior furnishings, landscaping and parking areas is approximately $75,000.

Activities for the year included Scout Week, Scout-O-Rama, Conservation events, Camporees, Explorer Survival Expeditions, Webelos Day and Explorer Expeditions. Council participated in the "Fit for Tomorrow" program with special attention in unit leader safety in many phases.

The year ended with 5,053 boys in the Scouting program. That included 61 Cub units with 3,092 boys, 64 Boy Scout troops with 1,647 boys and 18 Explorer posts with 314 young adults. They were assisted by 1,634 adults Scouters. Camping showed 50 troops with 713 boys and 98 leaders in attendance at Camp Alexander.

1963

Local Scout Council Invited to Host Jamboree….The Pikes Peak Council, Boy Scouts of America, has invited the National Council, BSA to hold the 1967 World Scout Jamboree in Colorado Springs. Ray Ryerson, executive director of the Pikes Peak Council said the 35 executive board members voted recently to send the invitation to national headquarters. "It will be the first time the World Scout Jamboree has ever been held in America," Ryerson said

The 1963 Jamboree was held in Greece. The Pikes Peak Council was host in 1960 to 60,000 Boy Scouts and adults at the 5th Boy Scout Jamboree. Ryerson said the type of facilities needed for the World Jamboree would differ considerably from that of the nationwide conclave here in 1960. *
They were not selected to host the event.

Activities for the year included Scout Week, Merit Badge Show, Conservation, Camporees, Survival Training, Explorer Ball, Encampment and Expeditions.

This was the kick off year for the new program "Scouter's Pot Luck Recognition Dinner" and over 1400 persons attended the event.

Pikes Peak or Bust Rodeo event with Scouts and actors Loren Green and Dan Blocker, most Scouts from Troop 18

Memberships at year end were: 62 Cub units with 3,211 boys, 67 Boy Scout troops with 1,739 boys and 20 Explorer posts with 294 young adults. 1,764 adults assisted with the Scouting program.

1964

Activities during the year included Civic Day, Scout-O-Rama, Camporees, Collections, and Webelos Day.

A record enrollment of boys registered in the Pikes Peak Council, Boy Scouts of America was shown at the end of the year 1964. In the Colorado Springs area, 86% of all boys between the ages of 8 and 17 years of age were registered in one of the three programs of the Boy Scouts of America. A total of 10,700 boys and adult leaders were registered in the local Scout Council during the past year. In the Fall Round Up for new boys, which started September 1 and ended December 31, more than 2,000 new boys were registered in the BSA program. Practically every one of the 157 packs, Troops and Posts registered exceeded its Round Up goals.

Every neighborhood in the seven counties of the Pikes Peak Council now has Cub Scout Packs registered. Funds for the administration of the Boy Scout Program in Colorado Springs area are provided by the United Fund, members of the 100 Club and sustaining members. The Cost of administering the Scouting program averages about $10 per boy per year. Boys pay their own way for attendance at summer camp, for their own uniforms and expenses incurred within their individual Packs and Troops by payment of weekly dues. "The Pikes Peak Scout Council was organized and chartered in 1916. For nearly 50 years the citizens of the Pikes Peak Region have shown the finest possible cooperation in helping to develop the nation's leading Scout Council here in Colorado Springs", Col Howard H. Cloud, Jr., President of the local Scout Council, stated.

Col Cloud, Council President

1964 6th National Jamboree, Valley Forge, PA attendance 52,000

Over 1700 to attend Scouter's Annual Dinner – The Annual Scouter's Pot Luck Recognition Dinner was a highlight of the 53rd Anniversary of the Boy Scouts. The dinner was held at the Broadmoor International Center and Gov. John A. Love would address Scout unit leaders, parents and community leaders at the Scout gathering.

Membership at year end was; 66 Cub units with 3,494 boys, 70 Boy Scout troops with 1,868 boys and 21 Explorer posts with 277 young adults. 1,797 adults assisted with the Scouting program.

1965

Five Pikes Peak Council Boy Scouts will leave Friday to serve as official delegates to the Boy Scouts of America World's Fair Scout Service Corps at New York. Scouts selected from the Pikes Peak Council are: Steve Blake, Post 1 sponsored by Broadmoor Rotary Club; Al Aberson, Troop 23 First Methodist Church; Howard Smartt, also of Troop 23 all from Colorado Springs and Terry Buol, Troop 38 sponsored by the Burlington Colorado Rotary Club and Floyd Shiery, Troop 55 sponsored by Arriba, Colorado Lions Club.

Ray Ryerson, Scout Executive said "that the Pikes Peak Council has been most fortunate in being asked to send a special delegation to the World's Fair Service Corps. The five Scouts selected are all high ranking and outstanding leaders of their troops and will reflect the importance that Scouting plays in the various communities included in the Pikes Peak Council."

FOUR SCOUTS HONORED — Eagle Badges were awarded four members of Boy Scout Troop No. 70 at Black Forest Community Building Wednesday night. Receiving the awards were (from left) Jeff Miller, son of Mr. and Mrs. H. E. Miller; Clyde Roe, son of Mr. and Mrs. Pearl Roe; Jim Shapleigh, son of Mr. and Mrs. E. E. Shapleigh, and George Stokes, son of Mr. and Mrs. William A. Stokes. (Gazette Telegraph Photo)

Activities for the year were; Scout Week, Scout-O-Rama, Camporees, Collections, Distributions, Webelos Day, Explorer Ball and 10 other Explorer Activities.

Membership at year end were; 8,158 boys, young adults and adults. The makeup showed 69 Cub units with 3,623 boys, 77 Boy Scout troops with 2,178 boys and 21 Explorer posts with 309 young adults. There were 2,048 adults assisting the Scouting program.

"The Sustainment Years"

1966 to 1975

1966

Today's Modern Scouts take to the Air – Today's Air Explorer Scouts learn techniques of flying in some of the world's largest planes. These Air Explorers of Squadron No. 1, sponsored by Ent Air Force Base are preparing for a takeoff training expedition in a "gooney bird." (C-47) Advanced "Air Exploring" includes training in nuclear physics and atomic energy.

TODAY'S MODERN SCOUTS TAKE TO THE AIR—Today's Air Explorer Scouts learn techniques of flying in some of the world's largest planes. These Air Explorers of Squadron No. 1, sponsored by Ent Air Force Base, are preparing for a take off training expedition in a "goney bird." Advanced "Air Exploring" includes training in neuclear physics and atomic energy.

Activities for the year included Scout Week, Webelos Day, Scout-O-Rama, Camporees, Collections, Several Explorer activities including Eagle Recognition at Scout-O-Rama.

Willis Magee presents patch to 1966 AdAmAn New Year's climb guest Explorer Scout Bill Bertschy. Scotty holds Bill's Scout qualification patches.

Membership at year end were; 69 Cub units with 3,704 boys, 78 Boy Scout troops with 2,193 boys and 23 Explorer posts with 316 young adults. Camping data showed 60 troops attended with 957 Scouts and 113 adults at Camp Alexander.

1967

"Church Service Honored – The Men's Club of the First United Presbyterian Church honored the church's service to Boy Scouts by presenting Troop 2 with a set of flags. C. W. MacNabb is Scoutmaster of the troop which is the first troop in the Pikes Peak Council to attain the half century mark. Boy Scout Troop 2 of the First Presbyterian Church will celebrate their 50th year of continuous charter during the month of October. The troop was founded in 1917 and Mr. E. B. Moore was the first scoutmaster of the nine boy troop. During the 50 years, Troop 2 has been enjoyed by 687 Scouts of whom 24 boys attained the rank of Eagle. Troop 2 is having a 50th anniversary dinner later that night which will be for all former Scouts and families".

CONSERVATION WORK — Three members of Boy Scout Troop 63 are shown here distributing the remains of 30 truck loads of Christmas trees in eroded areas in Palmer Park. The scouts and supervisors are (from left) Floyd F. Wohlgemuth, Scoutmaster; Phil Pettigrew, Duane Wohlegemuth, Bert Patterson, Pikes Peak Chapter of the Izaak Walton League; and Jim Kuenning. The Scouts are all Eagles, and attained that high rating because of conservation work in Palmer Park. Having residents put Christmas trees in Memorial Park for chipping and later distribution in Palmer Park was a joint effort by the Waltonians, Scouts and the City Park and Recreation Department.

Members of Boy Scout Troop 63 helped distribute the remains of 30 truckloads of Christmas trees on eroded areas in Palmer Park. This effort was an Eagle Scout project by several of the boys in the troop. Having residents put Christmas trees in Memorial Park for chipping and later distribution in Palmer Park was a joint effort by the Waltonians (Pikes Peak Chapter of the Izaak Walton League), Scouts and the City Park and Recreation Department.

First nighters learned Tuesday what scouting really is. Scouts of all ages performed on stage and displayed their wares at booths at this year's Scout – O – Rama at City Auditorium. The four night show is entitled "Scouting Rounds a Guy Out." Stage show includes Roman Ladders act by Explorer Scouts, speed pyramids by Cub Scouts, log sawing contest by Boy Scouts, Indian dance routines by Order of the Arrow Dance Team. Merit badge subjects from Aerospace to Fingerprinting were displayed in 124 booths. Many booths exhibit live animals. "The more that 280 Rotarians and business, professional and civic organizations serving as sponsors have added to the success of this year's event," said Claire Williams, chairman of the 1967 Scout – O – Rama.

Invitations were mailed to more than 400 Scouters and their wives for the 51st annual meeting of the Pikes Peak Council, Boy Scouts of America to be held at the Antlers Plaza Hotel. Major features of the program include a special musical program to be presented by the outstanding Boy choir of First Methodist Church made up of Cub Scouts and Boy Scouts. The annual report of council operations was presented by past president Robert G. Hibbard. The guest speaker was Judge George G. Priest, of Golden, Region Eight vice president. During the business meeting Scouters' wives took a conducted tour of the Antlers Plaza Hotel.

"Scouting Rounds a Guy Out" temporarily replaced "Be Prepared" as the motto of the Boy Scouts of America during Scout week. The week marked the 57th anniversary of the incorporation of the BSA in Washington D.C. on February 8, 1910.

Scouts made field trips to plants and offices to see firsthand what a particular business or industry does.

Activities for the year included Scout Week, Webelos Day, Scout-O-Rama, Camporees, Collections; Explorer Activities include Social, Vocational, Outdoor and Service Eagle Recognition at Scout-O-Rama.

Membership for the year was; 67 Cub units with 3,990 boys, 85 Boy Scout troops with 2,431 boys and 20 Explorer posts with 329 young adults. Camping this year showed 60 troops with 908 boys and 81 adult leaders in attendance.

1968

Joe Reich named to head Jamboree as its chairman for the 7th National Jamboree, and Gilbert Hesse as advisor to the Jamboree committee. The 7th National Jamboree was held July 16 to 22, 1969 at Farragut State Park, Idaho. Thirty seven Scouts and Explorers and three leaders from the Pikes Peak Council would attend along with 40,000 other Scouts and Explorers.

BSA Executive Board approves Coed Explorers…A few months ago it was reported that the Boy Scouts of America, was considering a plan for girls to join in its program for older boys known as Exploring. Now, it's official.

Activities through-out the year were Scout week, Webelos Day, Scout-O-Rama, Camporees, Collections, Distributions, Conservations, Courts of Honor, Scouter Recognition Dinner, Dinner for Junior and Senior High Newspaper editors.

At years end there were 70 Cub units with 4,083 boys, 84 Scout troops with 2,624 boys and 20 Explores units with 318 young adults. Camping on site were 62 units with 1,054 boys and 87 adults attending Camp A.

1969

Activities included Scout Week, Webelos Day, round-ups, Scout-O-Rama, Camporees, Collections, Distributions, Sponsor Good turns, Community Service, conservation projects and Explorer Camp. 1,348 Scouts and 99 Adult Scouters attended long-term Camping on Council Site (Camp Alexander).

Explorer Scouts (unknown date)

7th National Jamboree, Farragut State Park, ID attendance 35,000

Year-end numbers were 75 Cub units with 4,342 boys, 87 Scout troops with 2,807 boys and 19 Explorers with 338 young adults.

1970

View of Camp Alexander 1970

Membership at year-end was 92 Troops with 3,030 boys, 78 Cub Scout packs with 4,540 boys and 22 Explorer Posts with 359 young adults.

1971

George M. Gibson, Richard C. Sills, and John H. Alexander signed a deed for property along Uintah Street (East of our current service center) for the purpose of building a new scout service center. The land was formerly owned by the City of Colorado Springs and was purchased for $9,000. The land was presented by the trust to the Pikes Peak Council, Inc. Boy Scouts of America in consideration of one dollar.

1972

New Scout Handbook removes outdoor skill requirements for 1st Class; Improved Scouting program introduced; Operation Reach against drug abuse introduced

"The Boy Scouts are thriving," says Loren Swenson, the Council Scout Executive for the Pikes Peak Council of the BSA, from his Colorado Springs office. "We don't have as many members as we did in our peak years, the early seventies, but we are seeing the highest percentage gains in 30 years."

Membership gains haven't been continuous. Until 1972, when total Scout membership peaked at 6.5 million, the BSA had experienced only one year of declining membership in its 60 year history. Then a few years later, Scouting's stock plummeted. Between 1972 and 1979, more than 2.3 million members were lost.

"We weathered a few hard years in the seventies," says Swenson, who for 16 years has led the Pikes Peak Council, which coordinates the activities of 12,000 Scouts and adult volunteers.

Say goodbye to the old Boy Scouts. Come September they'll be known only as Scouts and many will be sporting bright red berets. The word "Boy" is being dropped because a two year study found that youth were being turned off by it, a Scout official said.

1973

"Former Executive Ryerson Passes Away --March 1973---On March 15, 1944, Mr. Ryerson became the scout executive for the Pikes Peak Council, Colorado Springs. He has served here for 29 years".
At that time, there were 845 boys registered with the BSA. In 1972, over 12,000 boys and girls were registered, plus 3,400 adults.
Two major developments that took place under his leadership were the building of Camp Alexander, three miles south of Lake George in 11-Mile Canyon, "one of the outstanding Scout camps in America." And the building of the Scout Service Center at 515 E. Uintah St., after occupying 10 different locations in 30 years. It was built in 1960.

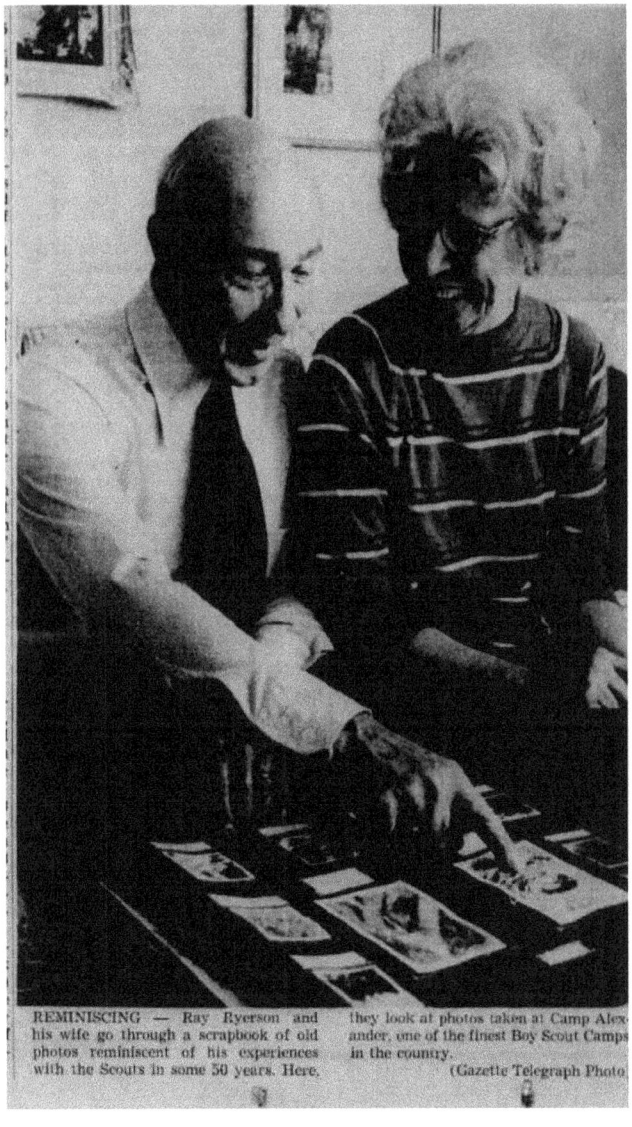

Mr. Ray Ryerson passed away in April 1977.

The first Council Wood Badge course (NC-11) was June 2-9, 1973, at Camp Alexander, with Clyde Wooten as Course Director. A consortium of Pikes Peak Council, Rocky Mountain Council and Santa Fe Trails Council consolidated staff to hold a week-long course and annually rotate the location among the councils. It was difficult for participants to commit a full week to training, so it was challenging to fill any course with the required thirty people.

Clyde Wooten

1974

BSA starts weekend Wood Badge course; First woman elected National Explorer president.

Story told to me at a church function. "Troop 247 from Colorado Springs walked to Camp Alexander from Colorado Springs completing their 50 miler hike".

1975

"Fueled by anti-establishment, anti-military sentiments of the late 1960s and 1970s, membership in Scouting plummeted, from 9,189 boys here in 1967 to 6,237 in 1975." *Reported by the Colorado Springs Gazette.*

"The Lean Years"

1976 to 1985

1976

BSA allows women to attend Wood Badge; women could now serve as Scoutmasters, Assistant Scoutmasters, Cubmasters and Assistant Cubmasters.

Wood Badge NC-109 held at Camp Alexander, July 31-August 1, 1976, Charles Mathews, Course Director.

1977

Eagle Scout Kevin L. Glover was selected by a special AdAmAn Club committee to join the organization's 55th annual climb up Pikes Peak New Year's Eve. In the traditional AdAmAn Club practice of adding only one member to the roster, annually, only one scout would be chosen.

Overwhelming competition for the coveted position and further liability issues, compelled the AdAmAn Club to withdraw the guest Scout positions.

9th National Jamboree, Moraine State Park, PA attendance 28,600.

1978

Local Council camps made available for family camping; Revised God and Country program announced; Age restrictions removed for severely handicapped Scouts; Outdoor skill reinstated for 1st Class rank.

1979

The Official Boy Scout Handbook reflects return of outdoor emphasis; National Headquarters moved to Irving, Texas

Wood Badge NC-127, 1979, held at Camp Alexander, Howard Cloud Jr., Course Director.

1980

New uniforms designed by Oscar de la Renta

50th anniversary of Cub Scouting.

1981

10th National Jamboree, Fort A. P. Hill, VA attendance 29,765

New Scoutmaster Handbook issued.

1982

OA Vice-Chief Kevin Moll, a 20 year old assistant Scoutmaster of Troop 66, chartered to St. Michael's Episcopal Church was selected as the 1982 National Youth Representatives of the Boy Scouts of America. Picked on a competitive basis from the 3.2 million BSA youth members he participated in the BSA 72nd anniversary celebration in Washington D.C.

Tiger Cubs introduced; The Cub Scout Leader Book published to replace five different leader books; The 1,000,000th Eagle Scout registered; Shaping Tomorrow project introduced.

1983

Below is a typical year's event from Troop 2, one of the oldest Troops in the council.

Started quarterly inter-patrol competitions, Order of the Arrow Dance Team, Annual trip to Bent's Fort for Koshare dances, 28 mile hike in Lost Creek Wilderness, Pheasant Patrol won Klondike Derby with perfect score! , 44th & 45th Eagle Scouts awarded, Hike up Barr Trail to hydroelectric plant for electricity merit badge, Fundraising: all-purpose cleaner, Service week in Rocky Mountain National Park, Troop 2 did Opening Ceremony for Olympic Sports Festival, Summer camp at Camp Alexander, The Pheasant Patrol won the Freezoree's Klondike Derby with a perfect score.

1984

Varsity Scouting launched -- BSA kind of picked the name "varsity" because it kind of conveys "the first string" The best you have.

Wood Badge NC-148, June 9-16, 1984, held at Camp Alexander, David Six, Course Director.

1985

Diamond Anniversary of scouting,

At least 600 boys and 200 adults are camping out this weekend on a 75-acre site in the former Johnson Ranch property near Chapel Hills. They have converged for a special, council wide camporee to mark the 75th anniversary of scouting. Order of the arrow Lodge 357 of the Pikes Peak Area Council of Boy Scouts is sponsoring the event. Don Shuck, lodge adviser, said, "Some 55,000 boys were at the 1960 National Jamboree, and now we get to hold a camporee and celebrate our 75th anniversary on the same site." There will be 40 demonstrations and exhibitions of sporting goods, outdoor equipment and college and military recruiters, plus an indoor rifle range in a trailer belonging to the Colorado Wildlife Department. The Saturday evening campfire will be the camporee highlight, they said, with skits performed by various troops and awards for the winners of the competitions.

11th National Jamboree, Fort A. P. Hill, VA attendance 32,615

"The Years"

1986 to 1995

1986

In 1986, the US Space Program had a major tragedy, the loss of the space shuttle Challenger.

All 7 of the crew were killed, including 4 crew members that had been scouts. Ellison Onizuka, a mission specialist, was an Eagle Scout.

On the mission, Troop 514 from Monument had a folded flag on board, which was lost at sea.

Nine months later in 1987, with the recovery of the wreckage, the flag was found in a locker wrapped in plastic. It was undamaged. The flag was declared the official flag of the US Bicentennial celebration. After the celebration the flag was returned to Troop 514. The flag is still in its possession and is used for significant activities in our area and around the country. It is only allowed to be carried by an Eagle Scout.

1987

Anti-Drug Campaign.

1988

First Scouting for Food program.

Pikes Peak has created Wood Badge Troop 1 for four events per year to encourage course participants to socialize and continue the example of Wood Badge leadership. The group meets the first Saturday of April to elect Patrol Leaders, July for a Service Project, October to meet new course participants, and an evening Feast in January with spouses. The council Wood Badge Coordinator is the Troop 1 Chair, currently Virgil Hoff II. Funds raised by a silent auction at the Feast are used for maintenance of a course supply trailer, special projects at Camp Alexander and scholarships.

Wood Badge NC-161, June 11-18, 1988, held at Camp Alexander, Virgil Hoff II, Course Director

1989

School Night to Join Scouting. Congratulations and thanks to all of you who helped make this year's School Night to Join Scouting Campaign the success that it was. Over 100 schools were opened and manned this year to allow over 2000 new youth to join our ranks.

12th National Jamboree, Fort A. P. Hill, VA attendance 32,717

1990

In 1990, Pikes Peak Council and the US Air Force Academy's Cadet Eagle Club joined together to develop one of the most successful recurring scouting activities in the history of the council - The Freezoree. There were 14 Freezoree's held on the campus of the USAFA. The first 5 (1991 -1995) were held in the cadet training area, Jacks Valley (far north end of the academy property). The rest were held in the football stadium parking lot (1996-2004). The move was required because Jacks Valley was becoming too small. The 1991 Freezoree I was a Rampart District event that had about 400 attendees. The Academy liked it and said they wanted to support a larger event. All the rest of the Freezorees were combined Pikes Peak Council and USAFA sponsored events. (Freezorees II thru XIV) The event grew to be the largest scouting event in the state (3,500 Cubs, Scouts and Adult Scouters), except for the National Jamboree. The Freezoree's were held on Super Bowl Weekend and we had a number of troops from out of council and out of state including 2 troops from Massachusetts. They were invited by cadets that were alums of the troops.

Early in the school year the Eagles Club would put a planning team together (mostly Eagle Scouts). The team consisted of about fourteen 3rd, 2d, 1st degree Cadets (sophomores, juniors and seniors), and one volunteer from the council as a mentor, historian and liaison between the cadets and the council. The cadet planners were from all over the country adding their unique ideas and experiences to the planned program. On the day of the event up to 200 cadets were added, to run the various events. The academy was overwhelmingly helpful in putting on a great event. (Annapolis and West Point put on similar events supporting scouting back east).

The results were tremendous. The cadets became human faces rather than a mass of unknown people on the hill; it was an excellent leadership/learning lab for the cadets and closer ties developed between the school and the community. The highlight of Freezoree X — it was run by 2 seniors that were introduced to the Academy at one of the earlier Freezoree's and decided to attend the Academy (becoming a pilot and a dentist).

The Jamboree District was established in 1990 and is named for the 1960 National Boy Scout Jamboree that was hosted within the district boundaries. The open space areas have long since been developed into neighborhoods and shopping areas many of us now call home yet we see reminders everyday of this major event in our local history. There are several streets and landmarks which are so named from this event (Jamboree Drive, Explorer, and Chapel Hills Drive are just a few.) Many local families are familiar with the Chapel Hills Mall but may not realize that it is located where the Scout chapels were during the Jamboree. Similarly, the "Briargate Mustangs" near the junction of Briargate Parkway and I-25 are very near the rodeo grounds and stables for that 1960 event. Today, Jamboree District serves the youth of School Districts 20 and 38 in the communities of Northern Colorado Springs, Black Forest, Monument, and in rural Northern El Paso County.

College of Scouting was held on 17 November 1990 with 21 Cub courses, 27 Scout courses, 7 Exploring, 8 Commissioner, and 10 General courses. Event was held at Pikes Peak Community College.

Mike Edwards, chairman for the Pikes Peak Council BSA 1990 Scout Expo, states that the Expo was held on Saturday, May 5, at the Widefield Mall, Widefield, Colorado. The theme for this year's Expo is "New Decade of Scouting."

In the fall, the Council had camporee down at Philmont Scout Ranch; it proved to be a success; however, the three hour drive proved to be intimidating and limited attendance.

There were 104 troops/teams with 1,957 boys involved. There were 116 Cub Packs with 4,958 boys and 39 Explorer Posts with 460 young adults. Also six Carrier Awareness Posts with 914 young adults restarted with a total of 8,289 youth involved in scouting.

1991

Learning for Life Introduced; Ethics in Action Introduced.

Recycling Really Works – The 48 members of Cub Scout Pack 81, operated by the USAF Academy, have run their recycling program for almost three years. They have sent more than 100,000 pounds of material off for recycling. The five hours of work each month have paid off in another way too: The Pack says it has pocketed almost $1,700.

November 23, 1991, Cub Pow-Wow held at Liberty High School, entry fee was $12.00 for Scouts.

The Council Training Committee approves design for a council-specific, light blue training scarf. This scarf would be worn by trained trainers at all training events "to build a cadre of trained trainers who are identifiable as resource people and should help enhance the value training."

1992

William "Green Bar" Bill Hillcourt passes away.

1993

13th National Jamboree, Fort A. P. Hill, VA attendance 32,000

Pike Peak Council adopts the American Red Cross CPR certificate for Scout certification.

1994

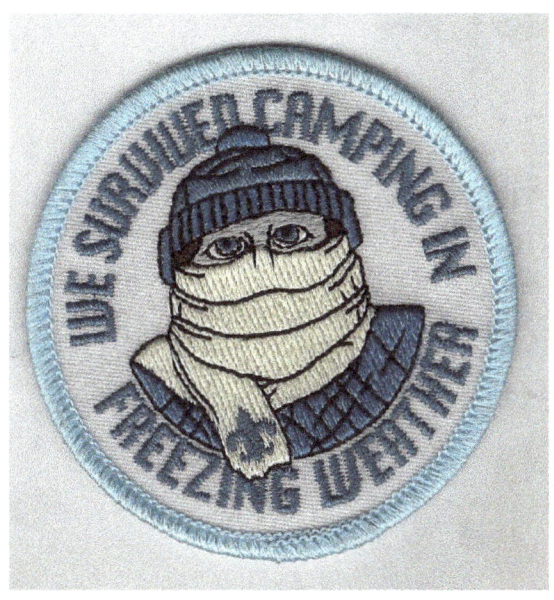

1995

The Frontier District comes from a rich and long history, reaching as far back as 1968. In 1995, two of the Council's districts, Silver Cloud and Rampart, were combined into a single district and the FRONTIER District was born! Its borders reached from the western mountain foothills all the way to the Kansas border.

Tenth College of Scouting was held January 21, 1995 at the Pikes Peak Community College. It was a six class-hour learning opportunity for adult scout leaders in Cub Scouts, Scouting, Boy Scouting, Exploring, Commissioner Science, and District and Council positions. "Degrees" were presented for completion of supplemental training in Cub, Boy Scouting, Exploring, Commissioner Science and General Scouting. The fee was $10, including course, class handouts, patch and diploma. Participants could choose from 57 course titles. Approximately 400 leaders attended.

"The Growing Years"

1996 to 2005

1996

November 2, 1996 was the date of the eleventh College of Scouting at the Pikes Peak Community College. The School of Cub Scouting offered 22 courses to select from, 21 in Boy Scouting, 8 in General Scouting and a Bachelor and Master of Commissioner Science. Entry fee was $10.00.

Scouts await the start of the "Chariot race."

A group of boy scouts compete in the "ski patrol" event.

Falcon Stadium was once again buzzing with activity Friday, as Boy Scouts from the Colorado Springs region began pouring in for the 6th Annual Boy Scout Freezoree.

In the previous five years, the Freezoree, a winter Boy Scout's Camp, was held in Jack's Valley, but because of the popularity of the ever-expanding event, it was moved to the stadium.

When Scouts and cadets awoke Saturday morning, with ice inside the tents, it was confirmed that the temperature had dropped to -3 degrees. Everyone was elated, until they had to crawl out of the warmth of their sleeping bags.

An estimated 1,810 Boy Scouts attended the event at Falcon Stadium this year.

1997

1997 was the first year that the Pikes Peak Council Summit Awards were presented to Cub Scouts, Boy Scouts and Explorers. The award was created to recognize boys, young men and women who have distinguished themselves in their scouting and exploring leadership and advancement endeavors; and set themselves apart in the areas of community service including religious involvement and leadership, as well as in school including academic record, leadership positions and club involvement.

Nominees were submitted from the scouting community and selected by a panel of scouting and community leaders. Finalists were selected regardless of age or level in the scouting program.

14th National Jamboree, Fort A. P. Hill, VA

The first weekend course held by the Wood Badge consortium (WE5-60-97) was August 23-25 and September 21-23, 1997, at Camp Alexander, Course Director David Haddock. Twice the staff had to set up camp two days early, but the new course had 39 participants.

1998

The 11th edition of the Boy Scout Handbook is published. Its first printing yields 750,000 copies, bringing the total circulation of the handbook since 1910 to nearly 36 million handbooks.

August 1, 1998, Exploring becomes the new Venturing Program. The name Exploring is now used for Learning for Life program. Venturing quickly becomes the fastest growing Scouting program.

Scouts collect more than 41 million cans of food to help feed the hungry.

More than 3,000 Boy Scouts from across Colorado and neighboring states of Wyoming and New Mexico came to the Academy Jan 30th for the 8th Annual Freezoree – a weekend of camping, learning and fun.

The Scouts braved cold weather, which dropped to a low of 10 degrees Saturday night.

Wood Badge W5-60-98 (1998) was a week-long consortium course, starting May 30th, Frank Collins, Course Director, 29 participants at Camp Alexander.

1999

Pikes Peak Council Friends of Scouting Breakfast was held in the Broadmoor this year. The guest speaker was Rick Barry. Rick Barry's professional career includes 10 seasons playing in the National Basketball Association, four seasons playing in the American Basketball Association, and more than 25 years in radio and television broadcasting. He also has coached professional basketball teams in the Global Basketball Association and the Continental Basketball Association. In 1987, Barry was named to the Naismith Memorial Basketball Hall of Fame, and in 1996, he was named to the NBA's 50th Anniversary All-Time Team.

2000

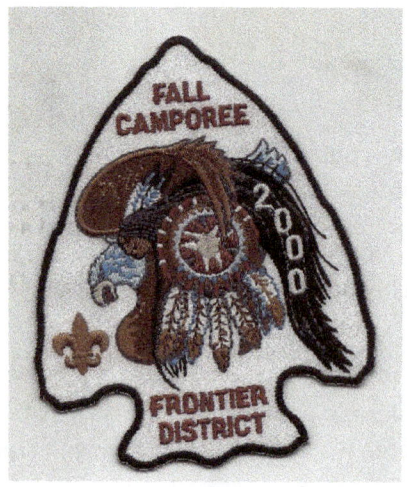

The Boy Scouts of America celebrates its 90th anniversary as the 100 millionth youth is registered.

2001

"Character Counts" was the theme of the November 10, 2001, College of Scouting held at the Janitell Middle School in Fountain. Twenty courses were available for leaders in Cub Scouting, 15 for Boy Scouting, 7 for General Studies and Den Chief Training. The Boy Scout Cooking Class always had the largest attendance. Fee was $15.00 and attendance was about 150 Scouters.

A newly revised Twentieth Century Wood Badge weekend syllabus was piloted in the council in 2001, August 24-25 and September 21-13, at Camp Alexander, Barbara Sweat, Course Director. Sixty-three registrants made this the largest consortium course ever. Despite the two weekends straddling the terrorist attacks of September 11, only three people were activated military. Sixty-one participants completed their tickets within the new shortened deadline of 18 months.

Falcon Stadium parking lot is the perfect place for a snowball fight, as more than 3,000 Boy Scouts found out over the weekend.

The Scouts, Scouters, Webelos and Explorers spent the weekend camping outside, learning about the Academy, earning merit badges and having fun. The boys viewed glider demonstrations, learned about model airplanes and saw working dog demonstrations. All the activities the youth enjoyed were organized by cadets.

First American Red Cross Wilderness First Aid Course approved for PPC merit badge.

On September 11, 2001, two commercial aircrafts plowed into the World Trade Center buildings changing the country and the way Boy Scouts would interface with military units in the area.

2002

At the Pikes Peak Council's 2002 Community Friends of Scouting (FOS) breakfast, held at the Broadmoor Hotel in Colorado Springs, more than 800 community and business leaders met the six most recent winners of the council's prestigious Summit Award; heard an inspirational message from U.S. Air Force Gen. Steve Ritchie, one of America's top air aces; and contributed more than $250,000 to the Council's Scouting program.

Trainer Development Conference held March 2, 2002, in Colorado Springs at the Junior Achievement World Center, Jeff Duncan, Chairman. This program replaces the Train the Trainer curriculum.

2002, August 5-11, the inaugural Wapiti Junior Leader Training Conference was held at Camp Alexander, David Deveau, Course Director.

2003

Wood Badge W5-60-03, August 18-23, 2003, was held at Camp Alexander, Dr. Donald Nelson, Course Director. The week-long course had 25 participants.

2004

Wood Badge WE5-60-04, April 30-May 2 and May 21-23, 2004, Course Director Donald Rabidoux. Although it was a Pikes Peak Council consortium course, it was held at Peaceful Valley Scout Ranch (Denver) because of Camp Alexander scheduling conflict. That was the earliest date of a Wood Badge course and participants endured snow! Of 28 participants, two were from Longs Peak and five were from Rocky Mountain Council.

2005

In July 2005, Pikes Peak Council moved from its four-decade home downtown to a temporary location in Office of the Bluffs on North Academy, Colorado Springs until the council's new headquarters at the intersection of I-25 and Fillmore Street was finished in July 2008.

Wood Badge WE5-60-05, August 19-21 and September 3-5, 2005, was held at Camp Alexander, David Deveau, Course Director, 29 participants.

"The Change Years"

2006 to 2015

2006

Lessons in law, government, and ethics DA's Office forms Boy Scout-related program

By DENNIS HUSPENI *THE GAZETTE*

What started as a handful of attorneys volunteering to help students prepare for a mock trial competition has blossomed into a full-fledged Boy Scout-affiliated post. The 4th Judicial District Attorney's Office recently formed Post 505, which will teach young people about the law and government and ethics, too. "Today's youth are tomorrow's community leaders," said Jerry O'Hare, program manager for the DA's Juvenile Diversion program. "We want to assist in their success." About 30 to 40 youths, ages 15 to 20, have signed up for the post, which was formed in December. "This is mainly for high school students who want to get a taste of what life as an attorney might be like," said Laura Crawford, Learning for Life executive. Learning for Life is affiliated with the Boy Scouts, but the new post is a Life program. That means it's open to male and female students. "It's open to all youths, regardless of gender, sexual orientation or belief in God," Crawford said. Learning for Life also runs Post 105 with the DA's Office. That post, in existence since 1998, is for young people who enter the Juvenile Diversion program. It's an intervention program for first-time offenders. Post 105 leaders teach job interview skills, good choice skills and how to avoid the dangers of drugs and alcohol. "The objective of our expanded juvenile programs is, quite simply, to turn kids around by improving decision-making skills and teaching community values," said District Attorney John Newsome. "The Boy Scouts of America, through its co-educational programs, is a valuable partner in reaching our objectives." About 1,480 youths have participated in Post 105, O'Hare said. "It's one of the best things we've done in years," O'Hare said. "I can tell you that between 85 and 90 percent of the kids who complete (105) succeed in our diversion program." O'Hare and Crawford hope Post 505 will be equally successful. In addition to preparing for mock trial competitions, students will be schooled in how government runs and ethics issues that govern how attorneys, judges and public officials operate. "Kids get a taste at an early age what it is like to be a prosecutor, defense attorney or judge," O'Hare said. "This can be a lifetime benefit."

2007

Wood Badge WE5-60-07 was a held at John Wesley Ranch, August 24-26, and Camp Alexander, September 21-23, Lee Rabidoux, Course Director. Twenty-nine participants included the first person (Jerome Sundee) to re-train because of Twentieth Century syllabus allowance.

2008

With the completion of the long-awaited building reconstruction, the new home of the Pikes Peak Council of the Boy Scouts of America opened for business last week at 985 W. Fillmore St. Originally a Bally's fitness center; the building interior was completely redone.

Still moving in and getting organized in the new, larger space, the council leadership scheduled a public grand opening September 27th. After October 1, the community will be allowed to hold meetings in the facility at no charge (as long as groups reserve in advance and understand that scouting events take precedence), according to Wendy Shaw, Assistant Scout Executive. "That will let everyone enjoy the great facility we have here," she said.

The location is the former Bally's gym, which was given new exterior touches while being gutted inside to make room for staff offices, meeting areas, storage, activity areas, a resource room/museum and the Hibbard Memorial Scout Shop. The 14,720-square-foot building also allows some room for future expansion, Shaw pointed out. From the parking lot in front, visitors can either go to the public area, including the store, or to the office side of the building in the two-story portion on its east wing. Space has been left for a climbing wall and shooting range that are to be added at a later date, she said. The meeting areas can be partitioned into four smaller rooms or one big area that can hold 218 people.

The council represents more than 11,000 Boy Scouts in an eight-county geographical area roughly bounded by Monument, the Kansas border, Pueblo and Hartsel.

The council headquarters had been on East Uintah Street for many years, but lack of space became an issue. Storage was a particular concern. "At Uintah, we had a Quonset hut," Shaw noted. She thanked Murphy Constructors, a Westside company which was the Fillmore project contractor, for doing a quality job.

In 2008, the Eagles Club was able to re-establish the tradition of WinterSpree where Cub Scouts met at the Air Force Academy for fun and games. The event had not been held since 2001 due to heightened security posture following the events on 9/11. The event was held at Falcon Stadium, in and around the press box. Nearly 300 Cubs from about 40 dens across the Pikes Peak Council, Boy Scouts of America, 200 parents and 80 cadet escorts participated. Indoor events included a demonstration of the Academy falcons, an orange balance on spoon race, a stretcher and three-legged race and a tug of war. Academy athletes sighed autographs and fielded questions. Outdoor events included a cadet physical fitness challenge, soccer game, obstacle course and Frisbee. Working military dogs from the Security Forces and the cadet Honor Guard drill team showed off their skills, and participants became acquainted with a glider and fire engine.

The WinterSpree events remained mostly unchanged between 2008 and 2012.

In 2008, the Pikes Peak Council acquired a beautiful parcel of land containing 200 acres just outside of Woodland Park in a gift from the estate of Leonard Johnson, Jr. The property is surrounded on most sides by the Pikes National Forest, and retains the character and beauty that Theodore Roosevelt saw when he visited the homestead. Glen Aspen Ranch is quickly developing into a quality facility for high adventure, advanced youth leadership training, and a center for adult volunteer baseline training to enhance Pikes Peak Council's continuing commitment to advancing and advocating the best training available for Scout leaders of all ages.

See attached history of Camp Aspen Scout Ranch.

2009

Scout 'college' draws 240 to Coronado High School: Despite cold and snow, some 240 Boy Scouts participated in a merit badge "college" at Coronado High School.

Cadets and Cub Scouts took to the field in Falcon Stadium for a day of challenges, learning and a lot of just plain fun during WinterSpree. Nearly 300 Cubs form 40 dens across the Pikes Peak Council, Boy Scouts of America, 200 parents and 80 cadet escorts participated. The event represented assets of the Academy and served to encourage Cub Scouts to continue in Scouting by providing examples of activities they can do with the skills they learn through Scouting.

Boy Scouts of America turned 99 in February. The celebration of Scouting's 99th year will continue when more than 70 Pikes Peak Region businesses and Scout groups showcase local Scouting at the 2009 Pikes Peak Council Scout Show, from 10 a.m. to 4 p.m. April 18 at the Phil Long Expo Center.

In years past, this event has garnered about 2,500 to 3,000 attendees, but this year expectations are high with improvements in programming and community involvement. The Boy Scouts are hoping to double their attendance this year. After all, it's a community event for a new generation of a movement almost 100 years old.

2009 was the first year that two Wood Badge courses were offered by consortium members, in two separate locations. WE5-60-09 was held at Camp Alexander, Ray Hoff III, Course Director, and WE5-63-09 was held at San Isabel Scout Ranch. With two locations, participants attended the closest course. Staff continued to be exchanged among the cooperating counsels, but effectively, the consortium rotation dissolved.

2010

Celebrating the Scout Centennial Colorado-Style 50 Years after Hosting the National Jamboree
By Rich Lieber, Pikes Peak Council Centennial Celebration Coordinator

2010 represents not only 100 years of Scouting in America, but also 100 years of Scouting in Colorado Springs, Colorado. An enthusiastic meeting of more than twenty boys and their parents was held on September 28, 1910 in Colorado Springs, and the first patrol was organized by National Commissioner F. John Romanes.

In 1960 on the Golden 50th Anniversary of the BSA, Colorado Springs had the honor of hosting the 5th National Boy Scout Jamboree. That National Jamboree still holds the distinction of being the largest National Jamboree to date with more than 57,000 Scouts in attendance. It was held across the highway from the newly opened United States Air Force Academy and at the time was more than eight miles north of Colorado Springs. Today, Colorado Springs extends well past the huge site which is now covered by shopping malls, homes and businesses. However, in celebration of our Centennial, on the same site where Scouts from around the nation once camped, we organized a Centennial Council Camporee on 50 acres of open land owned by Focus on the Family as well as a 2-day Centennial Scout Show at a nearby indoor arena. Distinguished leaders in our community who served on our Honorary Centennial Advisory Committee included our Vice Mayor, Better Business Bureau CEO, Chamber of Commerce CEO, the Vice Chancellor for Administration at the University of Colorado in Colorado Springs and our Colorado State Representatives.

Flags from participating troops ring the 100th Anniversary Camporee Site

With over 51,000 square feet of exhibits at the Scout Show, Packs, Troops and Crews demonstrated how they implement the five Scouting themes of Leadership, Achievement, Character, Community Service and Outdoors/Environmental Stewardship. Each family attending received a Passport to the five theme worlds (which when properly validated in each of the worlds made them eligible for additional chances for great door prizes). The Show was free to the public with the donation of a non-perishable food item for Care and Share (a local non-profit that provides food for the needy). We collected more than 1,550 pounds of food that weekend as well as monetary donations for Care and Share to purchase additional food.

In addition to sharing Scouting with our community, another aim of the Show was to capture the interest of youth in the community to consider post-high school education goals with an emphasis on science, technology, engineering and math (STEM). Higher education schools and organizations were present with hands-on STEM activities along with two aerospace companies that hire people with technical degrees. Members of the community even got to try their skill at docking with the International Space Station using a space simulator.

Other activities at the Show included our local zoo showing unique animals, our library district sharing historic moments in local Scouting, ham radio, leave no trace exhibits, knot tying and lashings, racing in Cubmobiles, and many other fun hands-on activities.

Docking with the International Space Station was one of the featured activities.

The Centennial Camporee featured a grand opening march of the campers led by members of the Fort Carson Mounted Color Guard on horseback.

Fort Carson Mounted Color Guard at the Centennial Camporee site with Pikes Peak in the background.

One highlight of the Centennial Camporee event was setting a world's record for the longest merit badge sash in the world. Scouts also had the opportunity to work on historic merit badges and attend the Scout Show, and they had their own fantastic arena show on Saturday night, all with a gorgeous view of the 14,110 foot Pikes Peak summit and the beautiful Colorado Rockies in the background. Our Centennial Celebration was an event to remember!

World's longest merit badge sash

In 2010 the first Council University of Scouting also celebrated the 100th Anniversary of Scouting. A wide array of scouting interests were available for adult leaders in Cub, Boy Scouts, General Scouting and Commissioner Science. University President, Daniel Lee, revitalized the program as part of his Wood Badge ticket. It was the first training to use electronic media (DVD) for course materials.

In 2010, the Eagle Club was able to re-establish the tradition of hosting the Freezoree at the Air Force Academy. The event was held in the woods near the Academy Preparatory School and was attended by about 450 Scouts from the Pikes Peak Council. The event highlighted instructions on survival skills in a scenario involving a plane crash in the Rocky Mountains. Activities included archery, fire-building, gully crossing, snares, water filtration, signaling and orienteering.

2011

With the disastrous events of 9/11/2001 hanging over our heads, the Freezoree's continued for three more years. Freezoree XV (2005), although planned and ready to go, was cancelled because of the increasing burden of security requirements and concerns for facilities and the people on the base.

Our 2011 Friends of Scouting Breakfast will be held on Wednesday, March 7th beginning at 6:59 am. Our featured speaker was Ron Young, former Iraqi Freedom POW, Eagle Scout, and finalist on CBS's "The Amazing Race". Ron credits his leadership role in Scouting and the training he received in the military for his survival after a 23 day capture by heavily armed Iraqi soldiers.

Lady Liberty Statue Returns To Springs City Hall
Copper Replica of Statue of Liberty

It was moved in 1999 for a City Hall renovation, and briefly relocated to the police operations center, but on Independence Day, a copper replica of the Statue of Liberty returned to where many residents believe is its rightful location.
"I didn't expect it to take eight years," said Stephanie Johnson, a community leader who spearheaded the effort to bring the statue back to City Hall. "I thought maybe three or four years, but not eight."

About 200 people attended a ceremony Monday outside City Hall to celebrate the statue's return. A fire department ladder truck unveiled the statue which rests on a new concrete base. Volunteers donated the effort and resources to restore the statue to its original condition and return it to City Hall.

Leonard Lemasany was among the Cub and Boy Scouts who raised money to present the statue to the city, and among four of those Scouts who attended Monday's ceremony. Lemasany said. "I do remember we sold newspapers to get pennies to build this."

The ceremony made an impression on a current Boy Scout. "I just feel it's a great honor to be able to do this," said Andrew Lee, 14. "Seeing the statue being unveiled, it was a great thing."

During the restoration process done by an expert in Fort Collins, several layers of paint were removed. Johnson said the paint began peeling while it was at the police center.

"And they also replaced the torch," she said. "Someone many years ago cut the torch off and put a light bulb in it."

Johnson said because a time capsule in the base of the original statue disappeared after it was moved in 1999, great care will be taken to protect a new capsule to be inserted at a later date and to record the items placed within. One of the items to be placed in the new capsule is a commemorative Liberty neckerchief slide, or bolo, that was made for Scouts in 1950.

Organizers said about 300 statues were made by a Chicago company in 1950 as part of a campaign known as Strengthen the Arm of Liberty to celebrate the Boy Scouts' 40th anniversary. Colorado Springs received the second statue made and only a dozen remain, organizers said.

According to a reference at Wikipedia.org, the statues when built were 8.5 feet tall, weighed 290 pounds and cost $350. Boy Scout troops in 39 states purchased the statues and donated them to their communities.

In 2011, the Freezoree was relocated back to Jacks Valley, named after Cleo and Zelda Jacks, who operated a cattle ranch in Jacks Valley from 1942 till 1954. The area has since been utilized for Basic Cadet Training. The event was held 25 – 27 February and included physical challenges, lashings, and confidence course obstacles. One of the logistical challenges for the event was gaining access into Jacks Valley through the secured entry control point, which cadets had to staff.

Wood Badge W5-60-11-1 was held April 8-10 and May 13-15, 2011, at Camp Alexander, William Bishop, Course Director, with 52 participants. The Training Committee elected to rotate the frequency of courses every 18 months to allow for alternating spring and fall Wood Badge.

2012

Springer fire -- Reported June 17, 2012, the Springer fire, in Eleven Mile Canyon south of Lake George, burned over 1,100 acres. Over 500 firefighters fought the fire. As the fire was brought under control on Sunday, June 24, 2012, resources were pulled from it to fight the Waldo Canyon fire.

In 2012 through 2014, the Freezoree continued much as it had in 2011 with some variations on the themes and activities that continued to revolve around winter survival and scout skills, and cadet EMTs were present to teach first-aid skills. In 2012 and 2013, the events were especially marked by high winds that presented a significant challenge because tents had to be pitched on concrete pads to protect the environment. In 2013, competitive elements were added, giving an award for the most spirted troop and an award for best adult leader cobbler.

Wood Badge W5-60-12-1, August 24-26 and September 14-16, 2012, was held at Lutheran Valley Church Camp and Camp Alexander, Douglas Meikle, Course Director, 28 participants.

2013

In 2013, the WinterSpree event was moved from Falcon Stadium to Arnold Hall due to facility schedule constraints. The Arnold Hall venue proved to be very successful and the Winterspree has continued to operate there ever since. While most of the event activities have remained the same, in 2014 the Eagles Club organized the event into four main activity areas in a round-robin fashion: Outdoor Physical Challenge, Scout Skills, Academy Showcase, and Science-Technology- Engineering- Mathematics (STEM) encounter.

The Pikes Peak Council welcomes and congratulates Cameron Ackley as the new Camp Director! We look forward to an exciting and fun-filled summer. Cameron grew up here and has been on the Camp Alexander staff for 10 years and is now one of our professional scouters leading the camp program.

2014

The Pikes Peak Council Boy Scouts of America holds an exciting FOS breakfast every spring to help offset the cost of scouting to our youth participants. This year's breakfast will be highlighted by Keynote Speaker and Pro Football legend Karl Mecklenburg.

In 2014, the Freezoree theme was once again established a scenario in which the Scouts learned winter survival skills to rescue a downed pilot. Activities included a station for building a small survival kit. The event again featured a competition based on points earned from the various stations. It also included an adult chili cook-off. Though the wind was much less severe that year, the snow was not. The snow was so deep that the Friday overnight portion was cancelled while the Academy coordinated a major snow removal effort to clear the road into Jacks Valley.

Wood Badge W5-60-14 was held at Camp Alexander, April 11-13 and May 9-11, 2014, Richard Trentman, Course Director, with 42 participants. PPC Troop 1 scholarships have been expanded to include youth registering for the National Youth Leadership Training (NYLT).

2015

The Pikes Peak Council of Boy Scouts of America has received a $50,000 Daniels Fund grant to support its ScoutReach Program, which helps low-income youth join Boy Scouts and participate in activities.

Since the early 1990's, the Pikes Peak Council has provided the ScoutReach program to meet the needs of all youth while providing a fun, safe and meaningful place to experience Scouting regardless of a young person's circumstances, neighborhood or economic background.

"These funds will allow the Pikes Peak Council to deliver rewarding Scouting programs to those who would otherwise not have the opportunity," Steve Ingham, president of the Pikes Peak Council Board, said in a statement.

New Adventure Cub Scout requirements introduced, and the first major overhaul of Cub Scout rank requirements in 50 years.

In 2015, the Freezoree returned to the Falcon Stadium parking lot to simplify the logistics associated with vehicle access, snow removal, and staking tents to the ground in high winds. The theme is "Jack Frost Klondike Derby", and featured ten competitive stations involving Scout skills related to shelter building, bear bagging, fire building, knots and lashings, first-aid, orienteering, leadership and teamwork, and totin' chips. The adults were invited to participate in a soup cook-off competition.

Wood Badge W2-6-15, 2015, was held August 21-23 at Camp Alexander and September 11-13 at Glen Aspen Ranch, Steven Hayes, Course Director, 40 participants. Glen Aspen Ranch is Pikes Peak Council's rustic property north of Woodland Park.

The PPC Troop 1 roster has grown to nearly 300 previous course participants, with about 120 people attending the Winter Feast. Focus of fundraising is on scholarships.

Attachments:

Council Camps

Camp Vessey

Skelton Ranch

Camp Alexander

Glen Aspen

Ha-Kin-Skay-a-Ki History

Council Camps

Camp Vigil

Camp Vessey

Camp Dreamland

Skelton Ranch

Cole Ranch

10 Mile Canyon

Camp Tarryall

Camp Carpenter

Camp Alexander

Glen Aspen

Since the beginning of Scouting, it was integral to the program's success to have long term outdoor experiences (summer camp). The first troops in the region temporarily used camps around the Pikes Peak area.

1918 - 1919 The first summer camp was held at Camp Vigil off Old Stage Road near Little Fountain Creek. This camp is now Broadmoor property on the east slope of Pikes Peak for customers of the hotel.
1920 The camp was at Camp Vessey, near Bear Creek Canyon.
1921- 1922 Camp Dreamland was held in the Black forest on the Cogswell property.
1923 -1925 Camp was held on the Skelton Ranch, 3.5 miles west of Woodland Park. It was 400 acres of an abandoned dude ranch.
1926 - 1928 The camp moved to Coles Ranch north of Woodland Park.
1929 - 1938 The camp was at Camp Tarryall near of Lake George. This was leased Forest service land. Some improvements were made.
1939 - Camp Carpenter west of Colorado Springs up the Old Stage Road.
1940 - 10 mile Canyon, summer camp was attended by 4 troops (71 Scouts) and held in 10 mile canyon.
1943 - Camp Vessey near Bear Creek Canyon. Camp Vessey was used for day trips and weekend camping till 50's
1944 - 1945 These two years the camps were held at the Colorado College's Geology Field Camp at Camp Ewing up near Woodland Park
1946 – Presently Camp Alexander is the year around camp for the council.
2008 – Glen Aspen open for Scouters use.

With the increase in usage of camps and growth of the Council over the years, it became obvious of the need for permanent camps for the Council.

Camp Vessey in Bear Creek Canyon

By Don Ellis

Camp Vessey in the 1950's

A number of maps show a "Scout Camp" in Bear Creek Canyon just off High Drive near the start of the Palmer Trail. If you go there today you will find a chimney from a burned cabin and a few remains of the former camp. This was once Camp Vessey.

The Colorado Springs Council of the Boy Scouts of America was established in 1916 and was one of the first three councils in Colorado. (The other two were the Denver Council formed in 1915 and the Greeley Council established in 1916.) In December, 1919 the Colorado Springs Council applied to the City of Colorado Springs for a grant of a tract of land in the Water Department's Bear Creek watershed where the Council intended to build a summer camp. This was only a few months after the Seattle Council opened Camp Parsons which was the first Boy Scout camp west of the Mississippi. So while Camp Vessey was not the first Boy Scout camp in the western United States, it would have been among the earliest. An article in the December 18, 1919 Colorado Springs Gazette described the proposed camp:

"The site is on a broad, level area, which is well wooded with pine trees. It is near a point where a small mountain stream submerges, and a good water supply is available, although the open stream does not flow through the camp. It is easily accessible from the Canon car and for that reason would be valuable as a week-end camp.

Plans for a bunkhouse, cook shanty, and the shelters necessary for a permanent camp are being drawn up ..."

The bunkhouse which was constructed had wooden bunks along the walls and was heated by a stone fireplace. In the 1950's there was no evidence that other shelters had ever been built. Water for the camp was supplied by a small cast iron pipe which carried water from the small stream a short distance up the canyon.

Camp Vessey was built by the Rotary Club and named for well-known singer Bernard Vessey. Bernard Vessey was a Rotarian who gained prominence in the organization and was later elected to be the Rotary Club's District Governor. He was also involved in Scouting; and had become a Scout Commissioner by 1929. So, it is almost certain that Bernard Vessey was instrumental in bringing the Scout camp into existence.

The time when the camp was actually built seems somewhat uncertain. A Jul 8, 1922 story in the Hutchinson News describes plans for Hutchinson, Kansas Troop 1 to spend a week at Camp Vessey. So, it seems that Camp Vessey had been built before the summer of 1922. Much more recent stories claim that it was built in 1923.

In 1925 the Colorado Springs Council merged with the El Paso and Teller Counties Council to become the Pikes Peak Council. The Pikes Peak Council seemingly continued to use Camp Vessey as a council camp until 1946 when Camp

Alexander was given to the Pikes Peak Council by J. Don Alexander (really Don M. Alexander his brother) of the Alexander Film Company. After 1946, Camp Vessey continued to be used by various Scout troops, mainly for weekend outings.

By early 1950's, the camp's water system had long been abandoned, probably because its shallow pipes had frozen and split.

At 6:15 in the evening on Saturday, April 7, 1962 the Sheriff's Office received a call reporting a fire at Camp Vessey. By the time crews arrived the cabin had been destroyed. Firemen from the Ivy wild-Cheyenne Canon Volunteer Fire Department stayed at the scene to prevent the fire from spreading to the surrounding forest.

Skelton Ranch

Skelton Ranch was located 3.5 miles west of Woodland Park, operated by and owned by Judge Willian T. Skelton and his wife, Lizzie Butler Skelton, along with a partner, Thomas Smiley. The resort ranch was located north of County Road 25, immediately west of Woodland Park and essentially surrounding what is now Tranquil Acres.

From 1917 to 1940 the resort ranch was largely vacant, although it was used for camping and outings. The Boy Scouts used the abandoned ranch grounds as an encampment in the 1920's

The following are excerpts from a firsthand account of a visit to the ranch that came from a Boy Scout from St. Louis, Missouri. Louis Chauvenet, a First Class Scout in Troop 8 from St. Louis, Missouri wrote an article for Boys Life Magazine about a 3 week visit this troop of 17 boys made to the Skelton Mountain Ranch in 1912. The following quotes reflect the experiences that anyone might have had at the ranch. About the trip up Ute Pass on the Colorado Midland Railway, he writes;

"From Colorado Springs we began climbing, and the grade was so steep that even a double header could scarcely pull our train of five cars over ten miles an hour. Beyond Manitou we entered the Ute Pass, which rapidly narrowed to a mere slit between two nearly perpendicular cliffs towering high above a small turbulent stream, with a road on its left bank and the railway, with its many tunnels, on its right. This pass is too narrow to be very spectacular, and its beauty was spoiled by a heavy thunder shower which lasted nearly all the way to Woodland, a distance of some fifteen miles from Manitou. When we were nearly at our destination we were delayed by landslides, but our commissary, who had handed out forty ham sandwiches at Colorado Springs, had unexpectedly produced a 'second installment' on the way, so we had no fears of starvation.

After several of these delays, between which the train ran no faster than a man could walk, we finally reached the small town of Woodland Park at about half past two in the afternoon. Here we were met by Al Akers, our future cook, with two wagons, on one of which we loaded our packs and the other, ourselves. Our scout master mounted a pretty little white mare, and the whole outfit set out for the Skelton ranch, some four miles to the northwest, where we arrived in spite of the fact that one of the bridges was washed out.

The country --- abounded in wild-flowers and plants which were mostly new to us, and the adjutant made quite a collection of them. The beautiful mountain columbines --- were out of season, but now and then a belated specimen was found in some sheltered spot.

---the most interesting trips made while in camp were those which took us farthest from home and required wagons to convey us.

The first of these was a journey of some twenty miles each way to the Petrified Forest and fossil beds. On the morning of this day we appeared at the ranch punctually at 6:50, having had breakfast and scoured the dishes. From there we started on two wagons, but the scout master rode on horseback with Judge and Mrs. Skelton and three other ladies from the ranch. The morning was fine and we were all in high spirits as we started in a southwesterly direction over high, rolling plateau, broken here and there by long, deep gulches, but commanding a good view of the Peak on the south, and a long ragged skyline far to the west. This view like that seen from the top of Solomon's Temple, is a sad one, for all the mountains have been ravaged by forest fires, and what was once heavy timber is now an almost open country, valuable neither for timber nor grazing. ---Before long we left the rocky, rain washed opening between the trees which the natives call a 'road', and struck a road in the real sense of the word – the Cripple Creek road --- we turned west --- and soon entered the tiny settlement of Divide. A freight train of about twenty-two cars passed through the town just ahead of us over a road on which the grade is so steep that the train had three engines – one in the front, one in the middle and one behind – and even then was not making more than ten or twelve miles an hour. After a short halt we took the road for the Petrified Forest.

--- About noon (we) stopped under a small, rocky hill, where a few evergreens were struggling for an existence. Here we alighted, and climbed to where the largest stump of the 'petrified forest' had been discovered. The earth and rocks had been removed around it (as its base is below the present level of the ground), and this stone giant stands about ten feet high and measures fitty-four feet in circumference. Three or four other stumps have been discovered.

It is safe to say that quite a few of us were disappointed, as the name 'forest' can hardly be applied to these few stumps, interesting though they are, and after we had been there but a few minutes a heavy rainstorm set in and served to dampen what ardor we yet possessed. After waiting in vain for it to let up, we took the road for Florissant (sic) with the rain rolling down our back and making little puddles under our ponchos for us to sit in. It was only a few miles to Florissant, which proved to be like Divide, a small settlement on the railway, but somewhat larger – boasting about two hundred inhabitants by our estimation.

---we hiked west along the railroad track for about half a mile to the fossil beds. These cover an area of nearly two miles and fossils are plentiful in a high bank through which the railway has been cut. The rock is easily broken off in this, flat pieces in the loose soil, and contains imprints of many things both vegetable and animal. Many of us found fossilized leaves and twigs, and would doubtless have found others had not the combination of a trainload of fossil seekers and another heavy shower caused us to beat a hasty retreat ---".

18 May 1924 – Newspaper article. Boy Scouts Will Camp at Skelton Ranch Again. Court of Honor to be held during encampment of June 9 to 21.

Clear, crisp mornings in the high woodlands and the mystic spell of the council fires are in store for more than 300 Boy Scouts of the Pikes Peak region who will attend the summer encampment at Skelton ranch. Ted K. Tillitson, scout executive, said last night. The camp will be the biggest for boys ever held in the region --- bigger in personnel, in equipment, in program and --- welcome news to the boys --- in kitchen and "mess" service.

Dining Room, Skelton's Mtn. Ranch   *Assembly Hall, Skelton's Ranch*

CAMP ALEXANDER AREA HISTORY

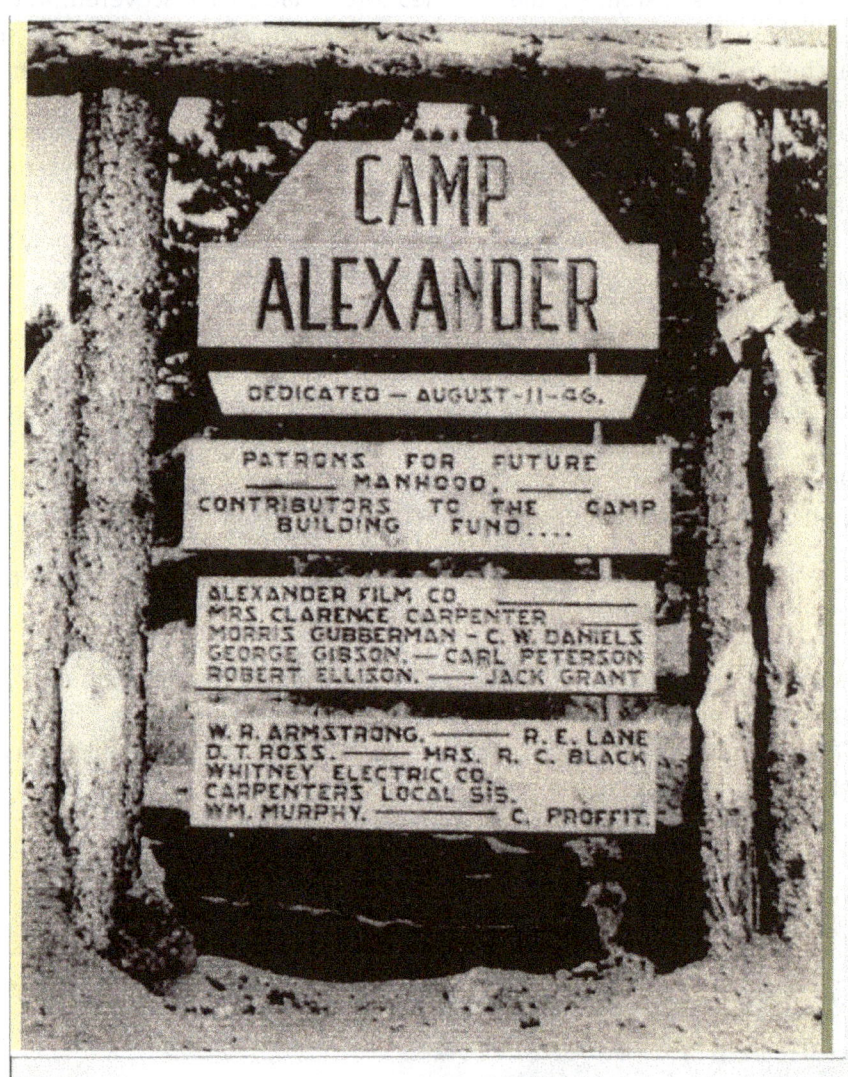

GEOLOGY

Why has Camp Alexander been such an incredible camp for so many years? Much of what a camp is all about relates to the location and what nature can provide for the program areas of the camp - the playing field. Therefore the geology of the area becomes important to the future success of the camp.

A long time ago (about 330 million years ago), the area where Camp Alexander and Pikes Peak now sits, was the bottom of the sea floor, and physically further south (about Mexico's latitude) than it currently is. Over time the land mass rose up from the sea floor and moved north, heading to its current location. The Rockies were formed during a mountain building phase called the Laramide Orogeny, 65 million years ago. This mountain building included Pikes Peak. The Peak is part of a rock mass that solidified from magma about 10 miles beneath the surface and pushed its way up as a solid mass. It is about 60 miles north to south and 40 miles east to west. This massive rock formation is called the Pikes Peak batholith. This mass is still slowly rising, but as in the past it is being worn down slowly by erosion. This erosion of the mass of granite back then has formed the basis of the shape that we now call Pikes Peak. Camp Alexander is on the western edge of this mass.

There is an ancient volcano field, Guffey Volcano Field in the South Park (Bayou Solado) area that erupted 35 million years ago. These eruptions formed lahar flows that created dams in the Florissant Valley forming a massive lake. The ash from some of the eruptions settled on top of the lake and trapped insects (area was more tropical than now) and forced them to the bottom of the lake. These insects' fossils became part of the Florissant Fossil Beds. It is one of four fossil beds in the world that contain insect fossils. Eventually the dams gave way and the lake self-drained.

In more recent years (150 to 20 thousand years ago) there were three known glacial periods; Glaciers, several thousand feet thick formed, finished and polished the land as we see it today.

NATIVE AMERICAN HISTORY

Whereas nature provides the playing field for the camp, history provides the personality and background. It gives a human element, and personality to the camp and surrounding area.

Earliest human history starts with people migrating from Siberia and eventually coming into this area. The first identified inhabitants we called the Clovis people. Following them, a new group called the Fremont people appeared, about 650 AD. They disappeared but probably evolved into the Ute Nations about 1250AD. This area became the Utes hunting grounds. The Utes were hunter/gatherers and called themselves the humans (Nuu-ci). They numbered in the thousands in seven separate bands. The largest band (Tabeguache, the people of the Tava (sun)) lived in the area around Pikes Peak, including the Florissant Valley. Other migrant bands of Native Americans passed through periodically. Around 1637, Spanish horses appear with the Utes, providing much needed mobility, for hunting and warfare. Chief Ouray was the leader of the local band of Utes and a friend of Kit Carson. Carson while trapping beaver in the Florissant Valley in 1852, observed a battle between the Ute and the Comanche over hunting grounds. Later the Utes were relocated by the US government in 1868 and again in 1880 and now live on the Utah border. They are now called the Uncompahgre Ute. These people started the long habitation of the Pikes Peak area.

POLITICAL HISTORY

This area of the country, when the Europeans became involved, was considered to be part of the Louisiana Territory (1763). In 1803 the land became part of the Louisiana Purchase when the US bought it for $15 million from the French. In 1861, the area becomes part of the Colorado Territory and in 1876 it was part of the 38th state, The Centennial State. It has had the Spanish, French, United States and Colorado flags flown over the land at various times.

In 1905, the forest surrounding the camp became part of the Pikes Peak Forest Preserve and two years later became the Pikes Peak National Forest.

EXPLORERS/TRAPPERS/TRADERS/PIONEERS

In 1806, a U.S. Army Lieutenant, Zebulon Pike, came into the area, surveying and exploring the newly acquired Louisiana Purchase for the US government. He and the survey party attempted to climb Pikes Peak (which he called Grand Peak). The November weather proved to be too big a hurdle and they did not succeed. The Utes called Pikes Peak/Grand Peak, Sun Mountain, but because of the popularity of Lt Pike and his writings the peak was named Pikes Peak and seemed to stick - for a while.

Pike's exploration party then continued on west to the area that is now Eleven Mile Reservoir and then south to the San Luis valley, He was captured by the Spanish as a spy and but later released. Eventually Gen. Zebulon Pike was killed during the War of 1812.

In 1820 another army topographic party, led by a Major Long, did climb Pikes Peak on July 14th, and re-named it James Peak, after a member of the party. The name however did not stick.

The 1820s and 1830s were the age of the mountain man and the beaver trapper in the Rockies. Riches could be had in beaver trapping. A plough (tanned beaver pelt) would bring $30 a piece, a month's salary in the flatlands. Colorado mountains and the Pikes Peak Region were relatively accessible and an ideal environment for beaver. Therefore many trappers moved into the area, including Kit Carson, the American Fur Company and Rocky Mountain Fur Company. Carson trapped with the likes of Jim Bridger, John Gantt and Old Bill Williams, famous trappers all. A favorite haunt was the Florissant Valley. Today up and down US 24, there is still evidence of many current beaver habitats.

In 1857, gold was discovered in the Pikes Peak region; and at Fairplay in 1859. These finds brought in a new influx of people, 100,000 men looking to strike it rich: "Pikes Peak or Bust". These finds were played out by 1863, but gold was rediscovered in Victor and Cripple Creek in 1890/91. These deposits are in a six square mile area that is the caldera of an ancient volcano. This area became known as "The World's Greatest Gold Camp."

A wave of new immigrants from Florissant, Missouri moved into the valley and started to build a town, (oddly enough to be named Florissant) in the 1870's. These new people started settling the area. Using the Homestead Act of 1872, a man named Charles Myron Shay homesteaded the land that is now Camp A. He farmed the land and raised produce, probably potatoes and onions.

This land in and around the valley was destined to become farmland and the little town of Lake George.

A settler, George Washington Frost, lost a fortune in cattle during the hard winter of 1886/87. He saw an opportunity to make lemonade from lemons. He built a dam in 1887, on the South Fork of the South Platte in the flats creating a shallow lake. He named it Lake Frost. The name changed over time to the Lidderdale Reservoir. When the adjacent town was large enough to change from a stage stop to a post office (1891), the lake and town's name officially became Lake George. Frost's money making idea was to let the lake freeze in the winter. He then cut and provided ice blocks for the railroad and the City of Colorado Springs and the Broadmoor Hotel.

RAILROAD

A growing population and businesses up Ute Pass from Colorado Springs prompted a need for a railroad versus wagons. The owners of the Robert E Lee Mine and Gipson Mine in Aspen started building the Colorado Midland Railroad (CMRR) up the Ute Pass in 1886. The rail extended from the roundhouse, currently 21st St and US 24, to Aspen and beyond. The railroad was built through Granite Canyon, now known as Eleven Mile Canyon, adjacent to the property of Camp Alexander. The access road to the camp along the river is part of the original railroad, along with the several tunnels. At the time a small village was built at what is now the entrance to Camp Alexander. It was built for housing the rail maintenance crews. It also became a stop for fishermen on the river. The village was named for the Governor of the Bank of England and contributor to the railroad, William Lidderdale.

The railroad was built with an elevation gain of 3106 feet up from Colorado Springs to Divide and drop down 1,112 feet to Lidderdale (8086 feet). In the distance between Colorado Springs and Lidderdale there were 8 stops along the 40.3

miles of track. The run took about two and a half hours for the passenger trains. The original intent of the railroad was hauling freight. Ore from the gold and silver mines in the area was hauled down to the Gold Hill smelter outside of Manitou Springs along with produce and ice for the city of Colorado Springs. Passengers, sightseers and fishermen were brought up from the lowlands.

In 1918, CMRR operations were stopped and the railroad was abandoned. The rails were torn up shortly thereafter. The rest of the canyon soon became impassable, then in 1932; Denver Water Company built the dam about 8 miles upstream from the future entrance of the camp. It took two years and $1.5 million to build the 135 foot high dam. This becomes the Eleven Mile Dam which backs up the South Fork of the South Platte River and forms the Eleven Mile reservoir.

CAMP ACQUISITION/DEDICATION

In 1944, Don M Alexander became president of the Pikes Peak Council of the Boy Scouts of America. At the time Pikes Peak Council membership was estimated at 3000 Scouts. A camp development committee was formed with Lester Griswold as chairman; Don M Alexander was Council President and Roy Ryerson was the Scout Executive. During 1944, a war bond drive was started to raise money to purchase property to build a permanent camp. In 1946, after a three year search of about 40 potential sites, the land for "Camp Rankins Gulch" was purchased from Carl and Pauline Berndt on January 17th, 1946. The Berndt's having bought the land in 1942 from C.G. Volz. Two portions of the property were also known as the "Marshall Ranch" on the north end and the "Clark Ranch" to the south. The camp included .5 mile of access road and the adjacent section of river. On the 8th of August 1946, the 340 acre camp was dedicated and formally named "Camp Alexander." The first camp had 44 Scouts in August.

The camp opened with minimal facilities: temporary dining hall (where the current flag pole array is), bath house, log living quarters (current business office), handicraft lodge (Carpenters Hall, named after the 2nd council president) and 4 campsites.

THE CAMP GROWS

1947, 378 Scouts are in attendance for the first full season. The camp was intended to be used the year around for various events. It appeared that the new camp was going to be a success. The original kiva was built on the ground of the current commissioner's row. It was donated by Frank Perkins and consisted of a small round wooden structure with vertical slats, some benches and a small stage.

1948, the first floor of the Elks lodge was built for winter use at a cost of $5000. The funds were donated by Elks Lodge #309 in Colorado Springs. This was followed by the 2nd floor in 1949 ($7500) for a permanent dining facility. The Elks Lodge was intended to be the finest of its kind on any Boy Scout Camp. Across the way, the medical lodge was built by the Lions Club in Colorado Springs for $5,000 to $6,000.

An important item that was missing for Camp Alexander was recreational water. Finally a 28 foot high earthen dam is put on the camp in 1950. It goes across Rankins Gulch Creek and forms approximately a 17.16 acre foot reservoir, - called Lake Hagnauer. The creek is its only source of water. It provided most of the aquatic activities for the camp. Eventually (1958), the swimming pool and original pool house are built at a cost of $40,000. In 1965, the lake dam had some maintenance done to it and was reinforced.

THE ALEXANDERS

The Brothers Alexander, Don M. and J. Don, started the Alexander Film Company in Spokane Washington in 1919. It produced ads and short subjects for the newfound movie industry. Five years later, in 1924, the company moved to Englewood, Colorado. There they expanded to include an aircraft production, Alexander Aviation Company. It was primarily used to build planes for the use of their film salesman. After a disastrous fire in 1928, Alexander Industries moved to the far northern outskirts of Colorado Springs. The aviation company was expanding and started building for commercial sales. It built the successful bi-wing Eagle Rock (one of which is hanging in Concourse B of Denver International Airport) and Eagle Rock Bullet (the first aircraft with retractable landing gear). These aircraft contributed to

Don M being elected as a member of the Colorado Aviation Hall of Fame. Both facilities, aviation and film making, were just north of the intersection of Fillmore and Nevada - much of which is still there and north of the power plant. The customer base for both aviation and filmmaking were nationwide and the films also became international.

In 1944 Don M. Alexander becomes the council president, using his business and organizational skills to make both the council and the new camp grow. He remained the council president for 8 years. Tragedy strikes in 1955 when J Don Alexander passes on. The J. Don cabins, on top of Cardiac Hill, are dedicated in his memory later that same year on July 7th. Don M was also selected to serve on the National Camping Committee. He received both the Silver Beaver and the Silver Antelope Awards for his contributions to the local and national Scouting programs. In February 1971, Don M Alexander passes away, ending an era but leaving an incredible legacy.

With the advent of television, the film company began to struggle when it didn't grow with the new medium. The company closed its doors in 1967.

CAMP ALEXANDER CONTINUES TO GROW

Major improvements for the camp were done by many organizations around town.

For example, after the summer season in 1968, the 52d Engineer Battalion, from Ft Carson, did an immense amount of maintenance for the camp. The battalion reroofed the buildings, developed water wells and trenched water lines below frost levels, built shelters for the shooting ranges, scraped and ditched the roads throughout camp, built a trailer camp with sewer lines and built a new greatly enlarged brick kiva. The engineers also constructed a new concrete porch on the second floor of the Elks Lodge, replacing the original wooden one. The engineers built the chapel, with a huge cross on the hill; the cost was donated by Mrs. Gertrude Alexander, the brother's mother. In 1969 the brick kitchen addition to the Elks Lodge was also built, with funds from Wharton Allen Estates. A rock climbing facility was added across from the pool house. All in all, much needed repairs, improvements and maintenance were accomplished and appreciated.

The current business office, in 1971, was the living quarters for the camp director and is thought to be a homestead building. It was remodeled and repaired. In 1972 volunteers built the storage facility and wall behind the kiva. The brick kiva has become one of Camp Alexander's trademarks, in good weather and bad. In 1972 camp fees were $30/week.

The Army (52d Engineer Battalion) again came back in 1984, and did some road work for the camp. The Nature Lodge (that looks suspiciously like a garage) is built out beyond the lake in 1986. It becomes one of the most used facilities in camp, offering the largest number of merit badges in any given summer. A new camp director's house was built between Oct 88 and March 89, leaving the old residence vacant for a number of years. Two additional pre-fab residences are built next to the camp director's house and across from Lidderdale during the summer 1996. These houses become housing for the Camp Ranger and family, guests and other "older" staff members.

When water became an issue in 1998, a new septic field, east of the pool and a water treatment facility near the old residence house (business office) were put in at the request of the state. The old bath house was proving to be inadequate with increased usage and more females in camp. The old one was torn down, a canvas shower was used for one year and the new bath house was completed (circa 2000).

The small trading post was moved from the small room on the first floor west end of Elks Lodge to the current trading post across the open field, greatly expanding its size and business capacity. The new trading post is thought to be the original dining hall moved here and was used for storage for some time. About the same time the acting business office was moved from the 1st floor of the east end of the Elks Lodge to the vacant old residence building (homestead building), the current business office.

The original Carpenter's Hall was refurbished (circa 2002) on the inside and made into a finely finished training center, Wooten Training Center at Carpenter's Hall ,named after a long time Wood badger, Scouter and Friend of the Camp A , Colonel Clyde Wooten.

At the lake complex, a new boat house was built with storage space and two outdoor teaching areas for use by the lake staff (circa 2007). This greatly enhanced the lake program and provided winter storage for the craft.

In 2007, the 50th Civil Engineering Squadron from Peterson AFB accomplished some structural repairs on our buildings and completed more road work.

Staff accommodations have become significantly improved. Two large staff bunkhouses were finished after some time delays while waiting for permits. They replaced approximately 15 two man tents. Each bunkhouse sleeps 16 comfortably, 4 each in four rooms. Expectation for the future is that two more bunkhouses will be built.

Over time, the camp has added significant facilities: three pavilions, (Order of the Arrow, First Class center and Fishing out near the river), a total of 15 campsites, several campfire rings for various uses; and an Indian encampment with teepees, out to the south of camp property. The OA ring was in this area and another was at a nearby large flat faced rock just to the north of the Indian village. Both of these OA sites were abandoned. The OA callouts now take place in the kiva. Three shooting ranges (.22cal, shotgun, and archery) have been built and improved by the Army.

A new ATV driving track is now on one of the former OA campfire rings.

During the winter of 2011, in an attempt to provide more off-season activities, an ice wall was built across from the climbing rock. Along with the usual winter activities, the wall has proven to be an immensely popular weekend winter success. The ice climbing program has been certified by National Council as alternate requirements for the rock climbing merit badge and was featured on the cover of Scouting magazine. This has added to the winter use of the camp.

A significant milestone was reached - the 7th session of 2013, the 100,000th scout attended summer camp at Camp Alexander.

A continuing concern finally came to a halt. The camp began replacing the wooden latrines. The camp is building new brick latrines with increased sanitation and privacy doors. The plans are for putting in 20 new facilities over the next couple of years, at a cost of $10,000 apiece.

In an effort to protect and centralize some of the maintenance and storage concerns, the camp maintenance yard is getting a large maintenance barn. It started after summer camping, 2015. It will house much of the maintenance equipment, vehicles and provide storage during the winter. There is some thought to adding summer merit badge programs in this facility.

MOTHER NATURE

Mother Nature still rules her domain. She does as she pleases and creates excitement where she goes. This part of the state has been going through a drought for maybe 10 years, depending on who you ask. In any case, our lake has had high and low levels for a number of years. However, during the summers of 2012-2014, the lake was low/dry enough to have to cancel the lake program. We instituted more activities on our portion of the river: kayaking, fly fishing, as an alternative. In the summer of 2015, the rain and snowpack got together and more than overflowed the lake, giving the lake a new and very welcome rebirth with all the old programs back in place.

The largest forest fire in Colorado history (138,000+ acres) started just to the north of camp across of US 24 in the 1st week of summer camp of 2002. It burned all summer and went as far as Woodland Park and approached Denver. It never came south of US 24 but did create some excitement.

The camp program lost a week and half during the summer of 2011, when a bout of bird flu came into camp. New campers who had just returned from a trip to Mexico brought it up here with them. A number of campers and staff came down with 2 day symptoms to the virus. The state asked us to close down and sanitize the camp.

Two fires during 2012 had an impact on Camp A. The Springer Fire, up Eleven Mile Canyon, came within a mile of the camp gate causing us to evacuate the camp at the direction of the county. It burned about 1200 acres north of the river.

Although not near the camp, the Waldo Canyon Fire affected the City of Colorado Springs all summer, and did close US 24 for some time, creating some concerns about access to the camp from the east.

Early in the summer season of 2014, a small tornado touched down in the trailer park across from the fire department in Lake George. It caused extensive damage to the RV Park but little else. The tornado was seen skipping along Lake George.

The end of the 2014 and all thru the 2015 spring, there was enough precipitation to refill our lake. It caused potential problems in Eleven Mile reservoir, requiring high levels of drainage down the river. This created some concerns and restrictions to travel, to and from the camp, for two weeks. Both the river and our lake were absolutely beautiful. With these issues, camp still goes on, creating some new excitement and adventures for all those involved.

CONCLUSION

Camp Alexander has developed and maintains an excellent reputation. Program is excellent and the staff always is highly regarded for its professionalism by the campers. The camp's nickname is Camp Awesome. This is very evident by the comments and by the number of returning units and the distances they come to be here. Out-of-council troops come from both coasts, with large numbers of troops coming from the surrounding states. Some have been American troops from Saudi Arabia. We have had an Irish Troop from just outside Dublin, Ireland referred by a Scoutmaster from Dallas. Scouts come a long way to be at our camp. We do and will continue to have an excellent program on an excellent stage.

Camp Mantra

"TODAY IS A GOOD DAY TO BE A SCOUT."

Compiled by Jim Yagmin

Glen Aspen Scout Ranch

History back to 1899

By Joshua Higgins, Life Scout

Nestled in the valley below the Woodland Park Reservoir, off of Loy Creek Road, Glen Aspen Scout Ranch is a 200-acre place of history. Owned by the Boy Scouts of America Pikes Peak Council, it is used for a variety of exciting events.

Glen Aspen Ranch has a history that dated back to 1899 and was acquired using the Homestead Act of 1862. The land started out as multiple properties and eventually, through many transactions, ended up as a giant ranch that was owned by Alex Cochran.

In 1906, a New Yorker by the name of Carl U. Fohn came to work for General William Palmer as a landscape gardener for Glen Eyrie. He was hired, most likely, because of his award winning gardens in New York. He continued to work for Glen Eyrie estate until Gen. Palmer's death in 1909.

Mr. Cochran, who bought Glen Eyrie, shortly after Gen. Palmer's death, now owned both Glen Eyrie and Glen Aspen. Mr. Fohn was rehired and continued to be the Gardner for Glen Eyrie until 1919 when he moved to Woodland Park, one year before the cabin was built on Glen Aspen.

Mr. Cochran transferred Glen Aspen ownership to his investment company. From that company, 200 acres was sold to Mr. Fohn in 1937 for $10. He had lived on the ranch for eighteen years as the caretaker for Cochran.

Through a sales agreement with Mr. Fohn, a portion of the Glen Aspen Ranch came to be in the ownership of the Leonard Johnson in 1938, again for $10. Through state parcel transfers, Leonard Johnson eventually owned the full 200 acre ranch. The Johnson Family used this ranch as a weekend getaway from everyday life.

On the weeks when they could not be there, they would allow their neighbors to come and use the ranch. Leonard Johnson Sr., who was the owner of the ranch, died in 1966 and divided the ranch between his children and his wife. Eventually, all the beneficiaries, except one, died and gave their pieces of land to the last beneficiary, Leonard Johnson Jr.

In 2007, Lenard Johnson Jr. died. In his will, he donated the 200 acres to the BSA Pikes Peak Council. The property came with the following conditions: the main cabin must be preserved, the property cannot be sold, no hunting or fishing is allowed on the property, no commercial tree cutting on the property, and the two donkeys on the property are to be cared for the rest of their lives.

When the Scouts took control of the ranch, it was in need of restoration. The caretaker at the time had neglected the land and was told his services were no longer needed. He left, but stole valuable pieces of the estate. Luckily, the family of the caretaker returned the pieces.

Under the care of BSA, the ranch was restored with fire mitigation, fixing of the cabin, needed construction repairs, and all around cleanup. It is watched over and cared for by volunteer camp masters." It is now used for scouting camping events, day events, and state events such as National Youth Leadership Training, all of which teach Scouts critical skills that will be used throughout their lives.

HISTORY of HA-KIN-SKAY-A-KI LODGE 387

Pikes Peak Council,
Colorado Springs, CO

HA-KIN-SKAY-A-KI LODGE #387 HISTORY

The Early Years

In August, 1946, the Order of the Arrow held their 14th (and last) Grand Lodge National meeting (in 1948 it became NOAC) at the air force base at Chanute Field, Illinois. Representatives of all the Lodges within Region Seven's jurisdiction attended the three day meeting. (Each region had its own jurisdiction at that time.) The objective of the meeting was to discuss the requirements to make the program of the Order of the Arrow meet the ideals of scouting. Attending this meeting was Harold Clark of the Pikes Peak Council. At the meeting he promised to bring the Order of the Arrow to every council in the Rocky Mountain area.

At the annual Council meeting of 1946, held at the Antlers Hotel in Colorado Springs, CO, the Pikes Peak Council Camping Committee stated that they were interested in the possibility of starting this new Order of the Arrow honor society. Since he was already elected as a member of the O.A. when he lived in Missouri, Clark was chosen to investigate bringing the program to Colorado Springs. He took his campaign to everyone he knew in the region.

Finally in March of 1947, the Executive Board adopted the Order of the Arrow as a program in the Pikes Peak Council. A slate of rules and regulations were adopted and charter members were selected. The lodge was officially chartered. At the recommendation of several prospective members, the first official meeting of the lodge was held at the close of the camping season on August 7, 1947. The new lodge would be called Pikes Peak Lodge 387. Harold Clark would serve as the lodge adviser. In the fall of 1947, the first Fall Fellowship was held and 27 new members learned about the Order of the Arrow.

In 1953, Pikes Peak Lodge 387 became known as Ha-Kin-Skay-A-Ki Lodge 387. The new name translated to "Big Sheep on the Mountain" and related to the resident herd of bighorn sheep on Pikes Peak. The name was reflected in their bighorn sheep totem.

Other councils in the service area of Region 8 had also formed lodges. They included the Denver Area Council, the Longs Peak Council, the Central Wyoming Council, and the Wyoraska Council. These lodges along with the Pikes Peak Lodge got together at Lowry Air Force Base in Denver as a part of the Scout Week celebration of 1951. They joined to form the Mountain Peaks Service Area. The first Service Area was 8A, which included the state of Missouri. It had four already active lodges from the very early days of the Order of the Arrow. Harold Clark had helped to start these Missouri Lodges from the Joplin, St. Louis, Springfield, and the Jefferson City Councils.

Charter Members of Ha-Kin-Skay-A-Ki Lodge # 387

Youth

Robert Lee Werner - Kit Carson, CO , Winningham - Burlington, CO, Penny - Burlington, CO, Don Darnaue -Cheyenne Wells, CO, S. Flatt -Burlington, CO, Su - Arapahoe, CO, Spears -Colorado Springs, Leo Oyler -Colorado Springs, Oyler - Colorado Springs, Oliver -Larnar, CO, Bernheim -Colorado Springs, Joe Clark -Colorado Springs, Bill Bignell -Colorado Springs, Larry Ash -Colorado Springs, Carl Peterson -Colorado Springs, Herald Walton -Colorado Springs, Everett Lentz - Colorado Springs

Adults

George Gibson Mike, Harry Rittenhouse Jim, Rudy Seidl, Gifford Theobald William, Harold L. Clark Wayne J., W.R. Martin, Jr. Bob, L.A. Walters, Guy R. McDowell Paul, Lester Griswold Gene, Don M. Alexander Robert

Section Changes

In 1944, lodges in Kansas and Missouri were split off from Area Q to form Area V. Lodges were later added to Area V as they chartered in Nebraska, Wyoming, and Colorado. In September, 1948, as part of the integration into the 12 Regions, the lodges of Area V (Region 5) were reorganized as Service Area 8-A (4 Missouri and 1 Kansas lodges), Service Area 8-B. (6 Iowa lodges) and Service Area 8-C (2 Kansas, 2 Colorado, and 1 Wyoming lodges). After Pikes Peak Lodge 387 was formed, it was placed in Region/Area V and Service Area 8-C. By1951, Area 8-C was divided between 8-D and 8-E. Service Area 8-C was disbanded and the Pikes Peak

Lodge moved into Area 8-E known as Tatokainyanka 356. 8-E remained in effect from 1951 until 1972.

Lodges included in 8-E consisted of Tahosa 383, Red Feather 403 (formerly Wiyaka tuta), Kola 464, Tupwee 536, Mic-O-Say 541, and Ha-Kin-Skay-A-Ki 387. In November 2007, the region decided to dissolve Section W- 5B. After the conclusion of the August 2008 cone/ave, Ha-Kin-Skay-A-Ki 387 was transferred to W-5A, while Tahosa 383 and Mic-O-Say 541 moved to W-5C. W-5A extended to southern New Mexico. As no elections were held at this event, each lodge was to attend their respective new section's conclave, where they were eligible to vote and submit candidates for elections. The proposed reshuffle of Area 5 for the end of August 2008 was superseded by the 2008 realignment.

To reflect the geography of Area 5, its sections were reorganized and renamed: Section W-5A ==> W-5 South; Section W-5C ==> W-5 North; Section W-5D ==> W-5 West; W-5B was dissolved on 08/25/08.

On September 1, 2008, W-5A became W-5S (south). The section now included Ha-Kin- Skay-A-Ki Lodge 387, Tahosa Lodge 383, Tupwee Lodge 536, and Mic-O-Say Lodge 541, all from Colorado.

Recent Times

As of 2015, Lodge 387 covers east-central Colorado, including Teller, El Paso, Elbert, Lincoln, Kit Carson and Cheyenne counties and is in Section W-5 South. W5-S includes Tahosa Lodge #383 of Denver Area Council #61, Denver, CO; Tupwee Gudas GovYouchiquot Soovep, Lodge #536, Rocky Mountain Council, Pueblo,CO; Mic-O-Say Lodge #541, Western Colorado, Grand Junction, CO; and Ha-Kin-Skay-A-Ki Lodge #387, Pikes Peak Council #60, Colorado Springs, CO. Chapters were tried early on, but were not effective.

Several national officers have hailed from the Ha-Kin-Skay-A-Ki Lodge. The lodge has also produced many section chiefs and section vice chiefs.

Several lodge members have been honored with the O.A. Distinguished Service Award. These include Dennis Downing and Kevin Moll in 1983, Christopher S. Belden in 1992, and Don Diaz in 2002.

In 2005 former Lodge Chief Andrew Sellers graduated from the Air Force Academy as the Top #1 Graduate in Academic, Military, and Overall Orders of Merit. In 2011 he graduated with a PhD in Computer Science from England's University of Oxford.

Twelve Arrowmen received the Arrowmen Service Award in 2002. The award is a national recognition program that honors Arrowmen for their service to the lodge, unit, and community.

Four members received the first year award and eight received the second year award. In 2005 ten members received the award, with four of them receiving their third year award. The Lodge 387 Ceremonies Team received the National Honor Ceremonies Team honor at the 2004 NOAC. (Only 10% of 250 teams received the honor.) In July 26-August 2, 2008, eight youth from Lodge 387 served on Arrow Corps 5 at Bridger-Teton National Forest in western Wyoming where they built trails. Three lodge adults served on staff. Arrow Corps 5 was a national O.A. Service project for the U.S. Forest Service. It served 5 different areas in the U.S. and was the largest service project in Boy Scout history with1200 participants.

Lodge 387 has received the National Quality Lodge award for the years 2001, 2002, 2003, 2004, 2005, 2006, 2008, 2009, 2010, and 2011. The Journey to Excellence award started in 2012 with three levels--Bronze, Silver, and Gold. Lodge 387 achieved JTE Gold level for 2012, 2013, and 2014.

The Ha-Kin-Skay-A-Ki Lodge performs service to the Council's Scout Camp Alexander on the order of upkeep, building, set-up/take down, and works on projects as proposed during their Fellowship Weekends, work days, and as needed as well as monetary donations. A separate camp at Glen Aspen Ranch is a major project for the lodge. Other service includes running scout camporees, helping with Cub Scout activities, collecting food for Care and Share, bell ringing for the Salvation Army at Christmas, cleaning up trash at area parks, and various other projects for the community.

At the Lodge 387 annual banquet, the Founder's Award is presented to a youth and an adult. It recognizes their outstanding service to the lodge and their personification of the spirit of selfless service. Lodge 387 presents its own annual award, the Rams Award, to one youth and one adult who demonstrate an exceptional level of service to the lodge and council in the past year. The new Vigil members are presented and the new lodge officers are inducted.

Lodge Patches and Flaps

The original lodge patches were simple and adequate in design. Scouts compete with their designs and now Lodge 387 prides itself in its unique patch designs. Newer designs have included a Colorado license plate, Garden of the Gods Park, the Broadmoor Hotel, a series from Star Trek, and a glow in the dark rams head. In response to the 2012 Waldo Canyon Fire that devastatingly affected Colorado Springs, the lodge released a fund raising lodge flap featuring a bighorn sheep looking over a burning area.

Lodge Newsletter and Website

The Lodge's newsletter was called the Ramshorn and was named after its totem, the big horn sheep. It was written, edited, and published by the youth members of the lodge. Three to four editions were printed and mailed to the lodge's membership annually. The Ramshorn switched to an electronic version in 2010.

In 2000 the Ha-Kin-Skay-A-Ki Lodge came into the modern world of technology when it announced its new website at http://www.homestead.comlLodge387/default.html. It later linked to the Council website at: http://oapikespeakbsa.org. In 2010 the Lodge went online with Facebook.

Written by: Diana Gantz

FOOTNOTES:,

1 http://www.OASections.com Copyright © 2006-14 by Robert Higgins. Effective: August 31, 2008

2 Mike Bliss, Western Region Chairman via Ken Hayashi, Western Region Committee

3 Ramshorn Newsletters, Ha-Kin-Skay-A-Ki Lodge 387, Pikes Peak Council~#60, CO., 1989-2009

www.ingramcontent.com/pod-product-compliance
Lightning Source LLC
Chambersburg PA
CBHW081325040426

42453CB00013B/2302